THE HILLS OF
CORK &
KERRY

The author on Mangerton's summit plateau with the Reeks in the background

THE HILLS OF
CORK &
KERRY

Richard Mersey

PHOTOGRAPHS BY
Bernd Thee

GILL AND MACMILLAN

Published in Ireland by
GILL AND MACMILLAN LTD
GOLDENBRIDGE · DUBLIN 8
with associated companies in
Auckland, Dallas, Delhi, Hong Kong, Johannesburg,
Lagos, London, Manzini, Melbourne, Nairobi,
New York, Singapore, Tokyo, Washington

5 4 3 2 1

ISBN 0 7171 1542 9

Published in Great Britain by
ALAN SUTTON PUBLISHING
BRUNSWICK ROAD · GLOUCESTER

Cover: MacGillycuddy's Reeks; photograph by Bernd Thee

Typesetting and origination by
Alan Sutton Publishing, Gloucester.
Printed in Great Britain by
Redwood Burn Limited

NE/110/1280–900/R/110287/4000

To my dear wife – Joanna

Contents

Introduction

In the subtropical south-west of Ireland rises chain after chain of rocky mountain. Eight peaks are over 3,000 feet high; 104 are more than 2,000 feet. The area is roughly twice the size of the English Lake District. But the charm of the area lies in its difference from the Lake District. There are no paths over the hills, no summit cairns, no people.

The inhabitants are mainly O'Sullivans, O'Sheas and McCarthys. They are far too sensible to climb over the hills except when they have to. Once I met a shepherd on the summit of Carrauntoohill. 'How often d'you manage to get up here?' I asked, bursting with enthusiasm. 'Too often', was the dour reply.

Hill-walkers neglect these mountains, perhaps because they are relatively remote. It takes six hours to reach them from Dublin, but twenty four from London. Perhaps, therefore, English walkers reckon that they can get to the Alps in the same sort of time and for the same sort of price. Perhaps that is why the Kerry Hills are empty. In any case, I do not complain. The emptiness, silence and majestic isolation of these peaks are their attraction. For instance, I have also spent two weeks in the 'last great wilderness' of Scotland: the Cairngorms. During that fortnight I met more people than I have met in a total of thirty five years walking in Kerry. If the Cairngorms are a wilderness then the Kerry Hills are the Sahara, which brings me to the weather.

Kerry, it is said, has little climate but much weather. Very true. The gulf stream gives Kerry warm, wet winters and warm, wet summers. Frost is rare, and the growing season is from 17th February to 6th January. It makes little difference whether you walk the hills in December or June. It is the fronts that make the difference, and decide your day. As the westerly air stream sweeps

1

in from the Atlantic it is forced upwards 2,000 feet or so for the first time since it has left the Caribbean, and as it rises it grows colder, condenses, and falls as a fine rain: what is known in these parts as a 'soft day'. 250 of the year's 365 days are 'soft'. The rain lasts on average three and a half hours, for the fronts move quickly over the hills. This bears out the Kerry saying: 'Any kind of weather seldom lasts more than half a day'.

The average rainfall is around seventy inches on the coast, but double that in the hills. Mangerton has recorded 140 inches. As well as the soft days there are the storms: 'The rain', says Boll[1], 'is absolute, magnificent and frightening. To call this rain bad weather is as inappropriate as to call scorching sun fine weather'.

The rain has certainly shaped the landscape. Without it Torc waterfall would be no more than a trickle, the river Inny a lazy stream and Glanmore Lake a stagnant pond. But there is much sun too; the weather station at Cahirciveen records an average of just under four hours a day, from a low of one hour in December to a high of six and a half hours in May.

The beauty of the Kerry Hills comes from the lightning changes in the weather. One moment you are trudging over foggy bog with sodden map and compass, and in the next instant the wind blows the mist into eddies, and shafts of sunlight cut through to illuminate a soft, shining landscape of myriad peaks, pools, and cascades.

Lloyd Praeger calls Ireland an amphibious country. He echoes Boll's[1] description:

> The whole west coast is indeed a country redolent of wind and rain, with an atmosphere that recalls blue eyes with tears in them: the only conditions under which it can look unattractive are in dry weather, with an east wind and that peculiar dispiriting grey haze that normally accompanies it. Better than that is honest rain sweeping in from the Atlantic, and the sea shouting on the rocks.

So he wrote in *The Way that I Went*,[9] published in 1937. The way that he did go was more considerable than mine. From 1896 to 1900 he did fifty field days a year as he listed Ireland's flora. Each field day was of twelve hours duration, and he tramped around five thousand miles in all. He sums up Irish weather with this verse:

> It ain't no use to grumble and complain.
> It's just as cheap and easy to rejoice;
> When God sorts out the weather and sends rain,
> Why, rain's my choice.

1. References are to titles listed on p. 155

The Kerry Hills are of old red Sandstone and were formed by the great Armorican convulsion of 300 million years ago. The convulsion was really a compression that gave to the kingdom of Kerry three gigantic corrugations. The crests are the peninsulas of Dingle, Iveragh and Beara; the troughs are the inlets of Dingle Bay and the Kenmare River. Originally, these hills may have been higher than the Himalayas, which are only 30 million years old and are described by Barrington[1] as 'no more than gigantic striplings'.

Time and the weather has worn down the Kerry Hills. The last ice age, which ended only some 5,000 years ago, has given them drama, in the shape of the coum. Most Kerry hills have a precipitous coum, or corrie, on their north-eastern flanks. The glaciers lingered longest on these sunless slopes, and as they inched down the hillside they took great chunks of it with them. Thus the retreating glaciers carved out huge ice basins. As often as not the basins contain a lake and sometimes there is a chain of these lakes, called paternosters due to their resemblance to the beads of a rosary. Beneath Brandon the paternosters number sixteen, but a more usual number is such as occur on a very typical Kerry hill – Mangerton (2,776ft).

Mangerton is typical because it looks so innocent whilst it is in fact rather dangerous. From a distance Mangerton seems to be no more than rolling upland; there is no hint of the Horses' Glen, a coum both magnificent and awful that cuts into its northern flank and boasts 1,500 feet of slimy cliff beneath the main summit. Picture yourself on top of this hill in mist and you will see the danger. There are no paths. The summit has barely a cairn and is hard to find in any event since the mountain is so flat. The wind and the rain will be worrying at your map and steaming up your spectacles. You will eventually choose a good compass bearing off the mountain, but others in your party will be utterly convinced that you are wrong, or that the compass does not work. They will indicate the opposite direction with conviction. Perhaps you will cross some bogland. To your horror you will see the marks of your own climbing boots already there, and one of your party is bound to say that you are going round in circles. In fact compasses work well in Kerry, so the moral is simply to carry two of them if you lack an iron will. And the other moral is, that it is always safe to go west, since coums face north and east.

Mangerton is a typical mountain. 5,000 years ago it was covered by a sheet of ice. The rocks in its coums have been worn down to a

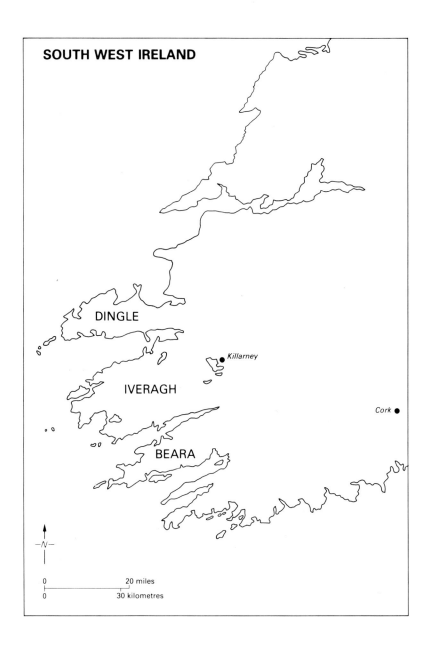

SOUTH WEST IRELAND

DINGLE

IVERAGH

BEARA

● Killarney

Cork ●

—N—

0   20 miles
0   30 kilometres

boiler plate smoothness by its glaciers – they are 'roches moutonnées'. But there are two oddities in the hills worthy of mention even at this early stage: the first is the area south of Lough Guitane which was once a volcano and therefore consists of igneous rock; the second is the land over 3,000 feet which rose above the ice sheet. The rock on these high ridges is different from any other rock in Kerry, for instead of being smoothed by ice it has been shattered by frost. It forms fragile nunataks, which look like the trolls of Norway. It occurs in MacGillycuddy's Reeks and Brandon Mountain.

In general the walks that follow start to the north or the east of the mountains concerned. These routes usually give the most exciting lines up the hills, and will normally include the circuit of a coum. Of course there are westerly approaches aplenty: the easy Saints Road up Brandon, or the Stations of the Cross up Knocknadobar are easy to the point of monotony. Indeed, a western approach up Mangerton appears so monotonous from the map that I have never attempted it. It follows, therefore, that, in mist, one compass bearing will not be enough. At least three will be required: to head of coum; across head of coum; down far side of coum. As well as bearings, timings are therefore important. Due to the varied nature of the terrain your speed can be anything between half a mile an hour and three miles an hour. Below I give some examples of typical Kerry going, with times and descriptions.

1. Open grassland. Example: the western section of the ridge of the Reeks. 3 mph.
2. Open grassland with bog bursts. Example: Eskatariff in Beara. 2 mph. The bog bursts are great trenches of sodden turf criss-crossing the high moorland, into which you must jump and out of which you must climb. The chances of landing on firm ground on the initial jump are good: nine times out of ten you will *not* shoot into the bog. The trenches themselves can open out into low-level plateaux, sometimes stony. All that is left of the original moorland in such areas is a few peat hags, but usually in an area of bog burst there is a choice between keeping high (jumping the trenches) and keeping low (walking along them). Whichever course you adopt will appear to you to be the wrong one. I have found the best general rule to be to keep high.

3. Alternating rock walls and grass ledges. Example: Hungry Hill, Beara. 1 mph. This sort of hillside is described locally and accurately as 'the benches'. It is a feature most common in the southernmost peninsula, Beara. It is naturally best to go along the benches rather than 'cross-bench', but the former is not always possible and the latter involves many scrambles up and down the rock walls, few of which exceed ten feet in height.

4. Pure rock. Example: Finneraragh, Iveragh. Generally smoothed into boiler plates by the old glaciers. As a general rule any rock that looks slippery is bound to be slippery, and any rock that does not look slippery has a fifty-fifty chance of being so. 1 mph.

5. Rock ridge. Example: Carrauntoohill to Beenkeragh. ½ mph. A proper airy scramble and good fun, though slow.

6. Scree. Example: Purple Mountain. 2 mph.

7. Boulder field. Example: north-west ridge of Beenkeragh. 1 mph.

8. Low-level boulder field covered with bracken, long grass, gorse and bramble. Example: lower eastern slopes of Torc Mountain. ½ mph. Very annoying country. Similar to the floor of the poisoned glen in Donegal, and also, I'm told, to the Falklands. Flies and midges enhance the irritation.

9. Valley fields. Example: anywhere. 1 mph.

I have included this last category and its very slow time as there is a tendency once back down amongst civilisation to think that all your problems are over. They are not. Kerry farmers build walls that are good for the job: keeping stock in. They make the walls fragile on purpose, for they know that a sheep will cross a sound wall but will shy away from something that will collapse under it. So the walls will also collapse under you, as indeed will most other types of fence and hedge. Most of them will in addition have deep ditches on one or both sides, sometimes concealed. A hill-walker at the end of the day is a relaxed but careless beast. Many is the wall I have seen toppled; many the straining-post snapped off at the base, and barbed wire wrenched downwards so that it no longer forms a barrier.

Somewhere there will be a gate out of the field, and it is worth detouring to find it, even though this takes time. A climb is after all, one long trespass really: all the land belongs to someone; even the top of Carrauntoohill. In a sense the hill-walkers are the guests of the farmers. This is just a simple plea to ask walkers to leave things as they found them. Hill-walkers in Ireland are utterly dependent on the good will of those who own the land.

I hope that the foregoing remarks about differing terrain show just how difficult it is to plan a walk in foul weather. How do you actually know, in mist, whether your speed is two or three miles an hour? How do you know when to change course? There will not be a marker cairn to help you. The answer must surely be to play it safe and do a low-level walk on a misty day.

They say that there are bold climbers and old climbers, but no bold old climbers. Well, I am certainly old, and some will say faint-hearted, but in my time in Kerry I have been 'pounded' (or cliffed) quite a few times too many. It is an unnerving and tiring experience to have to keep slogging back up the same hill in order to find a safe way off it. And there's also a problem with the maps of the area.

All maps were drawn by the Royal Engineers towards the end of the nineteenth century. The relevant sheets are 20, 21, and 24 in the half-inch series. These have contours at 100 foot intervals and considerable limitations. I rather doubt, for instance, that the engineers actually climbed the hills: there are lakes on summit ridges not marked at all; there are cliffs marked where there are no cliffs (e.g. at the head of the Dromochty Valley), and, worse, no cliffs marked where there are (e.g. the east side of Hungry Hill). So a route that looks straightforward on a map may not be so at all. In addition, the maps may mislead you on your approach drive, for the roads are given equal prominence though they have naturally changed greatly in the last 100 years. Some have been upgraded, others are now no more than green tracks.

The one-inch map of Killarney district has been somewhat modernised by the Federation of Irish Mountaineering Clubs; in particular, extra cliffs have been drawn in in the Reeks area. But this map only has contours at 250 foot intervals above 1,000 feet, so perhaps the half-inch are the more useful.

One other thing that the engineers did really rather badly was the naming of mountains. Any mountain named Coom (nadiha; nalassig) must be suspect, for 'coum' means valley. Indeed, most of the names on the map are not the local names at all, but for

The Head of the Cummeengeera Horseshoe – Bireca and Eskatariff

simplicity's sake I will, like others before me, use them in this guide. My favourite engineers' howler is the spelling of 'The Wood of the Berries', in Irish 'Fidh na gcaer', as *Vinegar*.

As an example I will give the same route over the hills described by Denny Shea, and then by someone reading it off the map. The O'Shea family should know the proper names, for that family has been in the area for at least a thousand years.

Denny Shea: Up over Streekeen to Cnoc na Bhfiacal. Strike west to Finaha and on to Motidu. South down over Eskatariff. East to Bireca then up over Bullawns and down over Toreenbaha and Foilcannon.

8

Map reader: Up over Cummeenahillan to Knocknaveacle. Strike west to the Tooth and Coomacloghane. Further west to KnockMichael. South over Eskatariff. East to Knocklarry, then up over Lackabane and Curraghreague, and down over King's gap, Wordsworth's Whorl and Foilemon.

From the last list of names it becomes apparent that I am describing the Cummeengeera Horseshoe, which must be the finest walk in Beara.

Beara

This is the southernmost of the three peninsulas. It is some thirty miles long and only nine miles wide, so all the hills dip into the sea and the walker is rewarded both by the majesty of the heights and the dreadfulness of the depths.

Beara, or sometimes Beare, is named after a Spanish princess who married Mug Nuadat, the first King of Munster. Earlier, Mug had fought and been soundly beaten by Conn of the hundred battles and Gol Mac Morna. Indeed Mug was only saved by the intervention of the Goddess Etain who changed the rocks near Kenmare into the likeness of soldiers. Whilst Gol and his men hacked away at these, Mug escaped to Spain where he met his wife Beara. Nine years later he re-invaded successfully.

From Mug is descended the great Gaelic family of the Eóganacht, to which the O'Sullivans, McCarthys and O'Donoghues belong. Should Queen Beara revisit her kingdom today she would find it not greatly changed. She would recognise the hills, lakes and rivers looking much the same as they did 2,000 years ago. She would, however, be surprised by the lack of trees, for in her day the whole land was clad in forest. The forests were felled by Sir William Petty in the seventeenth century for fuel for his iron smelting. His great rival, indeed the rival of every Englishman who set foot in this country, was the O'Sullivan Beare. He had strongholds in the castles of Ardea and Dunboy. Even today the visitor will find the surname O'Sullivan almost the only one in this peninsula; so much so that each O'Sullivan is called by another name to identify him: Jimmy the Master, Florrie the Dansel, Paddy Doorus, Teddy 'Nely.

1. Beara's Islands

This peninsula is steeped in history and legend, and no more so than off its westernmost tip, where three great rocks rear out of the Atlantic swell. They are the Bull, the Cow, and the Calf.

The Bull, or Teach Duinn, provided a wife for the great Fionn Mac Cumhail's court musician, called Cnu Dearoil. Cnu was a dwarf only four hands high. He wanted to marry someone smaller than himself, so Fionn found for him, on the Bull, a tiny woman called Blathnaid. Quoting Barrington:[1] 'Fionn took her, a fairy like Cnu himself, out of the Bull which was of course the other world, and the two little people were happily married.' The date is around A.D. 100. Could this couple be father and mother to all of Ireland's 'Little People'?

Today the only people who live on the Bull are the lighthouse keepers, and it is possible to visit it, along with the other rocks, by boat from Castletown, Garnish or Dursey Sound. I went from Garnish, to the north of the Sound, then through the Sound to the so-called sheltered side of Dursey Island. In the words of our boatman, it could not have been much calmer. As we approached the Calf we saw what he meant by 'calm'. The Atlantic swell surged mightily over the bottom twenty steps of the path up to the old lighthouse.

We did not feel like landing on the Calf so we sailed on to the Cow, a twenty minute journey. We swept through the eye of the Cow, a magnificent flying buttress of weathered rock to its south, and on to the Bull. The Bull also has an eye, much greater than the Cow's. It is a vast cave going under the very centre of the main rock. On the landward side of this cave is the 'landing place'. This is a vertical steel ladder. The technique is to wait till the swell takes the bows of the boat high up it, and then to jump for it. It is an interesting experience. Once ashore, we followed a series of steep steps and paths, and soon arrived at the lighthouse, with a helicopter landing-pad just below it.

Unlike little Cnu two thousand years before us, our quarry was birds, for here is a fine gannet colony. 1,500 pairs nest on the ledges. This, as colonies go, is rather small: the Skellig Rocks off Iveragh have a colony ten times the size, but the Skelligs are stiff with tourists, whereas the Bull is secluded and select. It is a haven for other sea birds too: kittiwakes, puffins, and Manx Shearwaters

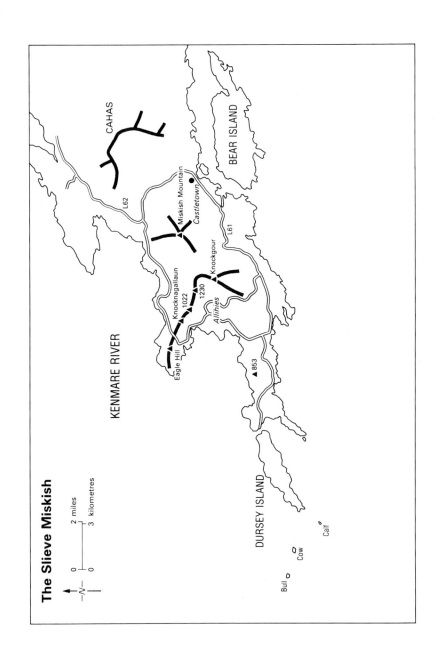

The Slieve Miskish

N

0   2 miles
0   3 kilometres

KENMARE RIVER

CAHAS

L62

Miskish Mountain
Castletown

BEAR ISLAND

Eagle Hill

Knocknagallaun
1022

1230

Allihies

Knockgour

L61

▲853

DURSEY ISLAND

Bull

Cow

Calf

all nest here. Each species has staked its claim on a very specific area of cliff. Those who trespass are quickly prosecuted.

It is an awesome experience to gaze on these birds perched on the last piece of rock before America. And your apprehension is further sharpened by the thought that it will be much harder to jump back into your boat than it was to jump out of it. At length we climbed down the steps and the vertical ladder. Our boatman, John O'Sullivan, was a real expert at driving his boat in on the swell, then backing away hurriedly as the retreating wave bared the rocks beneath the ladder. Each time he came in, one of us jumped. Soon our boat was full and John took us back along the north side of Dursey Island. We looked up at the Butter Cliffs, 400 feet high, and surely providing a few routes? But they too rise sheer from the sea, and surely to land at their base would be much harder than landing on the Bull.

Dursey Island itself forms the westerly end of the Slieve Miskish mountains, which stretch eastward to the Castletown road, whence they are dwarfed by the loftier Caha range. It is worth walking out to the end of Dursey. You cross the Sound by cable-car which leaves at predetermined but irregular intervals. Once on the island there is a road that goes through three hamlets. Beyond the westernmost of these juts Dursey Head. It is a dramatic affair with great spikes and spillikins of rock rising 100 feet sheer from the sea. Probably no man has ever set foot on them.

This is an eight mile round trip, so rather careful synchronisation with the cable-car is necessary, unless you wish to overnight on the island. The cable-car takes seven people, or fourteen sheep, or three cows, or a mixture of these. It works, naturally, on a first-come-first-served basis. If there are cows ahead of you in the queue they take precedence. Their need to cross may be greater than yours.

2. Beara West of the Castletown Road

The Slieve Miskish nowhere exceed 1,610 feet in height. At the very western end of the peninsula there are several dramatic knolls of a few hundred feet which plunge straight into the Atlantic and make a pleasant enough 'warm-up' walk if you have swum off the only true sandy beach in the peninsula: Garnish Strand.

Eight miles east of the strand is Miskish Mountain itself: a modest enough affair of 1,250 feet that takes forty minutes to walk up. It gives its name to the range – 'Sliabh' (Slieve) means peak and 'Miskish' means 'Standing on its own'. Miskish Mountain does just that. The view is far better than its modest height justifies: to the north, the Dunkerrons; to the east, the great 2,000 foot wall that marks the edge of the Cahas; to the south, the Fastnet Rock; to the west Dursey and the Bull.

Between Dursey and Miskish Mountain there is one rather fine longer walk. It lies over Knockgour and Knocknagallaun to its north, and is best approached via Allihies. As you travel away south from Allihies you will see above you a real stickleback of a ridge with many a steep face and gully dropping down to the old copper mines. This you will traverse after you have left Knockgour.

Knockgour itself is a very dull hill. It has a rough road up it and a TV transmitter at its top, which is flat. But do not despair; head due north for one and a half miles and you reach the stickleback ridge. This turns out to be quite broad, but exceptionally rocky and 'choppy' as they say in these parts: that is, a great many short sharp ups and downs of around fifty feet. The final ascent to Knocknagallaun is particularly steep, and the descent to the northern road from Allihies to Eyeries is over tumbled boulders.

This trip looks nothing at all on the map, but it took us five hours. Rather careful liaison is needed at the end of the walk as the northern road is quite a few miles away from the place where you left your car on Knockgour. It is, however, very easy for some of the party to drop down west from the col south of Knocknagallaun, pick up the vehicle, and drive it to the top of the pass between Knocknagallaun and Eagle's Hill.

As you traverse the ridge you look down on Ballydonegan Strand, which consists of man-made sand – the tailings from the old copper mines directly beneath you. These were started by the English planters, the Puxleys, who lived at Puxley Hall, near Castletown Bere, which was burnt in 1922 like so many other 'grand homes'. The Puxleys mined copper from the mid nineteenth to the mid twentieth century and at least half of the men of Castletown made a living from the mines.

It was, however, an earlier Puxley, John, who became involved in one of the classic trials of strength against the chieftain of the region, the O'Sullivan Beare. The whole story is told vividly by Froude in his 'Two Chiefs of Dunboy'.[3] This Puxley was an

14

eighteenth-century customs officer who took the proper but unusual course of trying to stamp out smuggling. This brought him up against the chief smuggler, Morty Og O'Sullivan Beare who lived in Coulagh Bay. He had here anchored a brigantine, a formidable vessel armed with eight guns, and more than a match for a naval cruiser. She was mistress of the Kenmare River. Morty's brig brought wine, brandy, and silk from France. John Puxley set about harrying Morty with his own cutter. His zeal was such that on Easter Sunday, 1754, Morty ambushed and killed Puxley on his way to church in Castletown.

The Dublin government condoned smuggling but could not condone murder. On a wild night in May they sent a force to surround Morty's house. Morty had just returned from France and his ship was at anchor below. The O'Sullivans bravely defended their home. Not until it was in flames around them could Morty be discerned and as he stayed shooting away in the inferno he was killed by a single shot. The English then sank his brigantine and took Morty's body to Dunboy. A few days later they dragged it behind a ship to Cork.

The O'Sullivan Beares had other, Irish rivals. These were the O'Sullivan Mors, who lived north of the Kenmare River. It was rivalry between the two families that split Beara up, in 1606, between the counties of Cork and Kerry. On the stickleback ridge you are wholly in Cork, but to your east the Kerry border slashes vertically through three-quarters of Beara in a most unnatural fashion. This is due to Sir Owen O'Sullivan (Beare) who took West Beara away from Kerry because 'the leading men of the County would not grant him the convenience of Assizes and Sessions in Killarney'.[1] This rather thin reason surely masks the real one: a desire to separate from the O'Sullivan Mors.

3. Beara between the Castletown Road and the Healy Pass

The largest and finest of the Cahas rise here, and their overall geometry is rather simple. There is a 'U' shaped cirque culminating in Lackabane, and, enclosing the 'U' on two sides, an 'L' shape reaching a zenith at Hungry Hill. There are three major coums that cut in typically from the north-east. Glanbeg, Glanmore and Cummeengeera are valleys as wild and wonderful as anything in Beara.

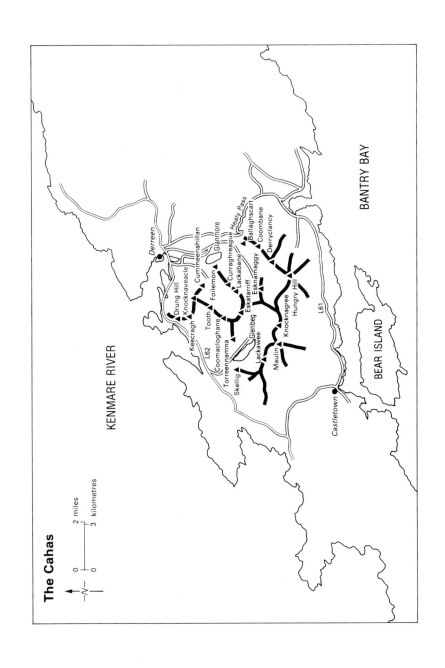

The Cahas

BANTRY BAY

KENMARE RIVER

BEAR ISLAND

Castletown

Derreen

Drung Hill
Knocknaveacle
Cummeenahillan
Glanmore
Curraghreague Healy Pass
Lackabane
Ballaghscart
Coombane
Derryclancy
Keecragh
Tooth
Foilemon
Eskatarriff
Esknamaggy
Knocknagree
Hungry Hill
Coomacloghane
Glenbeg
Maulin
Torreennamna
Lackawee
Skellig

L62
L61

N

0   2 miles
0   3 kilometres

Here I was baptised as a hill-walker. When we went on holiday at Derreen in 1947 I was thirteen years old. My parents did not know the name of any mountain save the 1,000 foot cone that rose behind Derreen House: Knockatee. Slowly my brother, David, and I identified and conquered the summits. Their height seems modest enough, today, but then, with David only nine years old, they were quite the highest things we had ever seen. We wore tweed suits and brown shoes. We had to be back at Derreen for lunch, on the dot of 1.15, and dinner at 8 p.m.

'The mountain across the bay', said my aunt Elizabeth, 'is called Keecragh. And the double mountain on its left looks like a back tooth. That's why it is called the Tooth.' And so I looked at the map, and tried to reconcile Elizabeth's information with it. Nothing made sense. Her 'Tooth' was surely Curraghreague and Lackabane. Her 'Keecragh' was Knocknaveacle. For the first time I realised that grown-ups were not always right. Soon I found the real Tooth, nestling behind the real Knocknaveacle, and the real Keecragh, a small spur away to the west of it.

We bicycled to the climbs in those days. Fortified by the fact that I already knew more about the hills than my parents, and feeling superior altogether, I proceeded to make every hill-walking mistake in the book. It was not long before I had led young David into thick mist on the (real) Tooth, to discover that our ideas about the right route off the mountain were 180 degrees at odds. Being the older, I won, but I was wrong, and after a wet and weary slog we descended into an unknown hanging valley. We scrambled and slithered out of it down dripping slabs and eventually reached the main valley floor, which we recognised as being the Cummeengeera Pocket. This was a terrible discovery, for we were two miles from our bikes, and we would be late for dinner. We arrived back at Derreen at 8.20. My father, furious, ordered us to bed dinnerless. But in the back regions of Derreen House lurked a good fairy in the form of Nanny. She had foreseen this crisis and siphoned off the remains of dinner as it went back to the kitchen. This she now revealed from its hiding place in her nursery cupboard, so we went to bed replete, but with an awesome respect for mist and the tricks it plays on your sense of direction.

It was here, amongst the West Cahas, that I grew to love, respect and fear mountains. Already, aged thirteen, I could see the romantic justification of Mallory's famous remark that Everest must be climbed because it was there. And from here I branched

17

out, in later years, to North Wales, the Lakes, Scotland, the Atlas, the Alps, the Himalayas. And as today I wander over the summits of Ben Nevis, Bidean, or the Matterhorn, my thoughts are always the same: these foreign mountains simply re-inforce my belief that the Cahas are the most magical mountains in all the world.

How exciting were those early pioneering days. We had soon conquered all that could be seen from Derreen, but I could see from the map that greater challenges lay beyond. To the west of Hungry Hill, for instance, were the two peaks of Maulin and Knocknagree. For three years they were just names on a map, but in the fourth year I saw their summits rearing out of the mist as we crossed the Healy Pass. And so we went to Glanbeg and climbed Maulin by a steep stone chute. And we went to the very end of the Glanmore Valley and set about conquering Knocknagree by the most complicated route. That day I must have been in an impatient mood, for I remember losing David as soon as we reached the plateau of the Glas loughs, and pressing on on my own in a manner most irresponsible. I made it to the top, but poor David was waylaid by a minor summit, trig. point 1519.

Those halcyon days of exploration were the most dangerous, due entirely to my lack of experience. We carried nothing – no map, no compass, no food, no waterproofs. We came off the mountains where'er fancy took us – and this practice led to another unforgettably unpleasant experience, which I will recall when I come to the relevant valley: Glanrastel.

But right now we are in Glanbeg and I must get back to my description of its magnificent hills. We are on the bottom of the 'L' that surrounds the 'U'.

Glanbeg is a valley black and bare. You get to it simply by taking the signed road at the top of Ardgroom's main street. 'Beg' means little, and once when I was back in London feeling nostalgic for the hills, I measured the lake and then drove to Marble Arch to discover how much of London Glanbeg Lake would cover. The answer is the whole of Hyde Park, Kensington Gardens, and a fair chunk of Mayfair. The valley walls of Glanbeg reach up much higher than the Hilton Hotel or Knightsbridge Barracks. On your left as you enter tower the mighty cliffs of Torreenamna, and on your right is Skellig, only 714 feet high, but a surprisingly stiff little one hour trip. In Glanbeg it looks no more than a pimple, but it is exactly the same height as the famous Skellig rock off Iveragh.

I have scrambled up the rocks of Torreenamna. It is a thousand

18

feet higher than Skellig, and after half an hour's 'sweat and blow' the angle eases and the stickleback ridge is most pleasant to traverse. But the mountain has a disadvantage; it has no top. After many a false summit you realise that Torreenamna is only a shoulder of Motidhu, which is 200 feet higher and one mile away. Motidhu (not marked on the map) is part of the Cummeengeera Horseshoe. Of course one can traverse on to it, and then further on over Coomacloghane, the Tooth, etc., to complete a 'half horseshoe'. That's a fine trip, but it will not suit you if your transport is in Glanbeg. You will probably swing south down coarse bogland to the valley floor again. This is a wet trip. I remember once counting the paces between each major stream. You have, you will find, a small fording problem every twenty steps!

The hillside beyond Torreenamna to the north of the lough forms the back of the Cummeengeera Horseshoe. It is a safe way off the shoe should you get into trouble, but, that said, it is not the sort of hill that you would want to walk up. In summer in particular it is covered with long grass that holds many a tick. Enervating country: and the crest of the ridge is much further off than it looks. This is a very typical westfacing shoulder – to be avoided.

To the south, behind Skellig, is the start of a fine seven hour expedition: the traverse of the 'L'. The route lies over Maulin, Knocknagree, Hungry Hill, Derryclancy, Coombane and Ballagh-scart. Its only disadvantage is that the main peaks lie south of the ridge, and so you must divert to reach the tops of Maulin and Knocknagree. Just after you have left Knocknagree you hit the eccentric Cork/Kerry boundary decreed by the O'Sullivan Beare in 1606, and a little further on, by the Glas loughs, is a road. Whither it goes I know not. It could not conceivably plunge down into the precipitous Glanmore Valley. Perhaps it is a turf-cutter's road. Around here you'll probably feel like lunch. The trip onwards over Hungry Hill to the Healy is described in the Hungry Hill section.

There is more yet to be described in Glanbeg. There is first the stone chute route up Maulin, seen very clearly from the cottages beyond the end of the lake. By those cottages, incidentally, are the greenest fields I have seen in all Ireland.

The chute, when you have puffed up to it, is sufficiently steep to make dislodged rocks a danger to the lower members of the party. Once out of it, you are on plateau and still a mile away from

Maulin's summit. The plateau curves gently, and traversing it must be very similar optically to crossing a small planet or moon. The horizon is never far away, but recedes with every step you take. There is no cairn on Maulin's top. This fact was known to the ill-fated John Puxley when he was traversing the hill in 1752. What worried him then was that he could see a cairn where no cairn should be. As he approached it, it looked increasingly human. Then he realised what it was: one of Ireland's hated middlemen, murdered and tied to a stake. The crows had plucked his eyes out. The crows, I suppose, might make a similar meal of a careless climber trapped on Maulin (the bald one) in mist, for once again there are no landmarks, and the route back down the chute is hard to find. There are cliffs to either side of it. Probably the safest bet is to head north-west to Lackawee, thence gently down to the foot of the lake.

The last route out of Glanbeg actually mounts the cliffs around the head of the Clogher Valley. These present no problems to children or grandmothers. At the top, 1,000 feet up, is the source of the Glanmore River. You simply follow the river along a valley so remote that you could be in another world. Eventually it tumbles over a lip of cliff and leaps down to Glanmore Valley in a series of magnificent cascades. The descent into Glanmore is easy enough so long as you keep the river on your left. The Clogher traverse is only an hour and a half and very much an outing for all the family, half of whom will, with a bit of organisation, have driven a second car to the head of Glanmore and will be traversing the valley in the other direction. And so when you meet them you exchange keys. In fact I have always found it quite safe in these parts to leave your car unlocked with the keys in it.

A car left at the head of Glanmore is particularly safe, for you will park in the farmyard of Florrie the Dansel (O'Sullivan) – a fine figure of a man. Florrie has few possessions apart from his sheep, which he grazes in Clogher. He has put up pieces of plastic on poles by the river to deter his sheep from crossing it and drowning. Once, after a very heavy storm, which of course makes the cascade that much more magnificent, I found Florrie facing catastrophe. His sheep, thinking in their simple way that the far bank of the river had to be drier, had all swum it. And every one of them had been swept to its death over the cascade. 'These must be hard times Florrie', said I lamely, to which he replied, chuckling 'Aye,

Glanbeg Lough from the head of the Clogher Valley

but there have been good times too.' Florrie had so little, and had lost what little he had. Yet he could laugh it off. The farmers of Kerry have so much to teach us so-called 'civilised' town people.

We are now in Glanmore Valley, so I will describe the walks out of it. Knockagree (1,929 ft) is best tackled from here. It has a finer summit than Maulin or Hungry Hill, and is one of the very few mountains that stands out from across the waters of the Kenmare River. The view is fine for the height, though bigger hills block it to north and west. In order to avoid a boring 'out and back the same way' it is an idea for the faster members of the Clogher party to nip up and down it during the traverse.

The tiny Esknamaggy (878 ft) at the head of Glanmore sticks a fine

Esknamaggy – A low level scramble

prow of cliff out eastwards, and this makes a good scramble on days when the cloud is down. The route off it to the south plunges down a near vertical grass gully. You lower yourself hand over hand by the tussocks.

On the east side Derryclancy, Coombane and Ballaghscart are not really worth doing in their own right, and on the west both Curraghreague and Lackabane would feel almost insulted that you had tackled them from behind.

The main climb out of Glanmore is Hungry Hill. This mountain is also called Cnoc Daod, and, by those to its south, Angry Hill. It is

2,251 feet high and is the crown of the Cahas both in altitude and in shape. Just as a crown has hard vertical sides and a soft flat top, so does this hill. Every approach to Hungry Hill is up steep rock until you reach the 2,000 foot contour. There you gain, as it were, the velvet of the crown – one square mile of cushiony turf. The mountain looks ungainly from afar. Perhaps it was this shape that caused Dr Pochin Mould[5] to write this unforgivable insult about the Cahas, which it pains me to quote:

> The pattern of the Heights is rather of monotonous repetition of rock and boggy moorland in rounded massive haunches, with a certain majesty like the hindquarters of an elephant, but seemingly hardly worth the individual climbing of each.

You cannot see the top of Hungry Hill from Glanmore Valley; indeed, the very first time I climbed it I went up Derryclancy by mistake. You simply weave your way through the many waterfalls pouring down its northern flank and either scuttle up the steep little rock faces, always wet, or the plentiful vegetation that divides them. Lately some Belgian students have marked a route up with orange arrows, but they are not really necessary as there are no serious cliffs hereabouts.

It is half a mile from the 'lip' of the crown to the summit cairn, and another half mile to the south top, with a second cairn and a better view. If you descend by the same route you will find the rock faces quite troublesome, as cliffs are invisible from above. However there's always a way round them, and the whole trip will take two and a half hours.

It is more interesting to walk over the tops to the Healy Pass (which forms the horizontal of the original 'L' described under Glanbeg). As you leave Hungry Hill's summit plateau you will traverse down across some of the most spectacular benches in the Cahas. There is a temptation to veer south towards Coomadavallig Lake, as that way you go with the benches. But it must be resisted, as there are mighty cliffs to your right.

After traversing the northern col and puffing up Derryclancy it is worth looking back at the apparently sheer rock face that you have just come down. Along the Derryclancy Coombane ridge there are two sizeable lakes not marked on the map. These are somewhat disconcerting to come across in mist, but in fact it's all straightforward enough from now on down to the pass. The whole trip takes three and a half hours.

Hungry Hill from Coomgira

I derive a certain smug satisfaction from seeing the tourists leaving the comfort of their cars on top of the Healy, and scrambling up Ballaghscart (The Mountain of the Pass). They think, poor souls, that they will gain the summit in ten minutes. They cannot know that the first proper summit is three miles away and 1,500 feet above them.

The best way up Hungry Hill is from the east. You cross south over the Healy and turn left at its end towards Castletown. Then you take the second right, just over a bridge, into Coomgira. Hungry Hill rises above you in two great tiers of cliff. Indeed it looks angry; and I checked with John O'Sullivan who lives in the second last cottage, who confirmed that the proper name is Angry Hill.

We walked up on to its southern spur, 1,000 feet high and a little boring, but then we gained the rock and it was grand going. There are splendid friction slabs with minute corrugations like corduroy trousers. Up these we scrambled for forty minutes or so and suddenly we were at the southern summit cairn with a bang. Then, good springy walking over Angry Hill's soft centre to the main summit, and, mist descending, rather hurriedly off it over the acute benches of its Derryclancy face. As anyone can see who climbs Angry Hill from this side, there is no easy descent before a broad shoulder leading east off Derryclancy called (confusingly) Derreen. And so we traversed over Derreen and then walked under Angry Hill's great eastern cliff face, black except for the waterfall that boils down it from Coomadavallig Lake. These precipices are not marked on the map at all.

The route took us four hours.

Angry/Hungry Hill may be the crown of the Cahas, but it is not the crown of climbs. That lies three miles to the north: the Cummeengeera Horseshoe.

To reach it you turn south off the Castletown road as it crosses the bottom of Kilmakilloge Harbour. You can then either press on to the foot of Glanmore Lake and take a track through the woods, or, better, turn right again only half a mile after you have left the main road and leave your transport near a concrete bridge over the Driminboy River. You are now under Cummeenahillan, properly called Streekeen.

The natural line up Cummeenahillan is behind you. It is up the northern spur of Reenkilla and looks like a splendid rocky scramble. To the west of that the valley of Cashelkeelty seems to give the easiest stroll up the hillside. In both cases the appearance is deceptive. The Reenkilla ridge is 'cross-bench' at its worst, and the valley is long, dreary and wet. The best way up is straight out of Cummeengeera. You simply strike north from the road and struggle through gorse and bracken to the bottom of one of several benches. Then you haul yourself up the long grass. It is indeed a nasty enough start to the climb, but it is all over in twenty minutes and you're sitting on one of Cummeenahillan's three summits looking at the route up Knocknaveacle, which looks just as

Hungry Hill. South summit and corduroy slabs

punishing. But it is not – it is an easy and airy walk. There is a handy sheep track to the north.

Knocknaveacle has four summits widely separated. None have cairns, but the furthest is the highest. From it you will see the western spur of Keecragh with a shoulder stretching down to little Drung Hill and Knockfadda. These peaks are not part of the horseshoe, but make a little trip worth doing on its own on a bad day. (You start at Collorus, traverse the first three tops and then find yourself on entertaining rock ribs running up to Knocknaveacle. The best way down is due north to a stone circle above a wood. That's a choppy descent with many a jump down a rocky bench.)

But the horseshoe route lies south now, and as you leave

Knocknaveacle you must scramble down a thirty foot wall which is a good landmark in mist. There is an insignificant knoll between Knocknaveacle and the Tooth, quite rocky, and the odd 300 foot scramble up the Tooth is as rocky as you care to make it. If you keep left there are a few optional slab and chimney problems. The English sappers clearly muddled names here, for Knocknaveacle also means 'the Hill of the Tooth'. The Tooth (1,945 ft) has a top rocky and flat with many a sparkling pool to quench your thirst.

Onwards to Coomacloghane is the easiest section of the whole walk – a good time to light up the Afton Major if you have the habit – but the descent from Coomacloghane is cross-bench again, very like Hungry Hill and slow work. All the time you have a mystical view out to the Atlantic and the Skelligs. I've done this walk in most conditions, snow included, but perhaps the most dramatic was one blustery April day in sun and hail. The storms stung our faces so much that we had to walk backwards. Still, I prefer spring hail to summer midges, and that hail had the added bonus of starting way out to sea. Great shafts of black joined the ocean to the clouds and as one of them swept towards us a hailbow formed before it. The colours had twice the intensity of a rainbow; yet the storm was only a few hundred yards wide and so there was no arch, just one dazzling strip of colour on a black ground.

Between Coomacloghane and Motidhu there are some optional pinnacles, in truth hummocks, which any purist wishing to do a proper horseshoe should include.

Motidhu (the Black Sod) has neither name nor height on the map. It is the westernmost summit of the shoe and is like all others on it, just under 2,000 feet high. From here onwards you travel over heath-land with bog burst. You are on the high ridge of Eskatarriff, though indeed this is an odd name for a ridge, as it means 'The Path of the Bull'. It is hard to strike up any sort of rhythm hereabouts, for you are forever jumping down into boggy dykes. There are a minimum fourteen jumps, I have found. By the law of averages you will only plunge through the crust on two of them.

To your south the ground slopes away quite tamely to Glanbeg, but to the north is a good cirque of cliffs dropping down to the house of a murderer, of whom more later. Those cliffs are at their most dramatic at Bireca, a needle of a peak east of Eskatariff. Its north face is nearly vertical for 500 feet. You could scramble down the col between it and Eskatariff with no problem; indeed that's a

Cummeengeera Horseshoe. Looking towards Lackabane from Coomacloghane

good thing to do if the weather goes rotten, as the walk out of Cummeengeera is dramatic indeed.

There are two major peaks left on this shoe: Lackabane and Curraghreague. The walk up to them is pleasant enough as there's a fair sprinkling of rock pavement. The summit of Lackabane is typically hard to find, yet it is, at 1,984 feet, the summit of the whole walk. Indeed if you define a peak as a summit with at least 500 feet of descent on all the sides, then Lackabane is the only peak on the shoe. All the others are just tops. The trip on to Curraghreague takes ten minutes and you pass some fine fluted rock columns. Though fourteen feet lower than its neighbour, Curraghreague has the best defined top on the whole circuit.

The narrow ridge that plunges off this hill to Torreenbaha (1,200 ft, not on map) is hard to find in mist. The compass will indicate it, of course, but your commonsense may override the compass. The obvious shoulder off this hill leads towards the Glanmore Valley and a five mile road walk back to your car with, behind you, no more than a half-completed horseshoe. The next most obvious shoulder leads over cliff into the mouth of the Pocket. You can contour the mountain back to the proper route this way, but it adds an hour.

The proper ridge is the middle ridge. It is steep and narrow, rock and heather. There is another temptation, once you have got down to the col at 1,000 feet, to descend the easy looking gully to its north-west. This is a loathsome declivity of gorse and bracken. It is better to climb up Torreenbaha, which only takes ten minutes, and then to continue east along the top of the spur to Glanmore Lake. There are several minor knolls on it with, surprisingly, cairns on their tops.

Once you reach Foilcannon (on the map Foilemon, 931 ft) you must plunge off the ridge northwards. This is bad ground: slimy cliff and long grass which conceals many a boggy hole. A high wall helps to start with; you can walk along the top of it, but after that you slither and curse and aim for a standing stone on the valley floor. Once at the standing stone you have half a mile back to your car across the valley. There's many an awkward fence and ditch for you to fall into; indeed I do not believe that I have ever crossed these fields without plunging into something at least knee deep. But that doesn't seem to matter at the time, for I'm at peace with the world after a splendid walk.

The Cummeengera Horseshoe is only six miles, yet it can easily

The North face of Bireca

Fluted rock on Curraghreague's summit ridge

take six hours to complete. The terrain is tough, and the total ascent could well be 4,000 feet. Our family record is held by my youngest brother, Andrew, who took three hours fifty four minutes, running some of the way, and having his lunch on the move.

Naturally you can also do the circuit from Glanmore Lake, but that route is a little worse for morale in the early stages as the steep blow up Foilemon is only a prelude to a bigger blow up Curraghreague; whereas if you start up Cummeenahillan you've just got twenty minutes of hell and that's it.

If the weather is too bad for the horseshoe it's worth walking up the floor of the valley. You'll see some inviting cliffs on the east side of the Tooth. I went up these once to rock-climb with my wife. It was not a very good trip. The rocks are broken, rotten, and vegetable, as indeed are most of the cliffs of Kerry. The only clean rock face in this valley is the vertical prow of Bireca, and that is too daunting for me and, so far as I know, unclimbed.

Betty Healy and Frank Windser describe a route above a tumbledown shack at the head of the glen in their 'Sandstone Hills of Cork and Kerry', *Irish Climbing Journal*, 1955:

> Above the shack there is a colossal slab – the Sheep King's Mantle. We climbed it by lines of weakness near the left hand edge. But a magnificent route could go straight up the centre of the slab in two ninety foot pitches on (one hopes) continuous tiny holds, without any chance of protection and but little of return.

The authors have this to say about Kerry's sandstone:

> This rock provides magnificent scenery and fine ridges, but it has many disadvantages from the climber's point of view. Although some of the cliffs are 2,000 feet high they tend to be broken into smaller buttresses and faces which, though often substantial in themselves, get lost in the environment. They are often wet, the lines of weakness choked with vegetation, and the almost ubiquitous lichen makes them extremely unpleasant for vibrams under wet conditions (nails are good). Lines of weakness usually tend towards the horizontal, so that climbs are usually discontinuous with escape routes at the end of each pitch.

That quote supports my own view. Kerry rock is nasty scrappy stuff to go up, but much nastier to get stuck on coming down.

The road up Cummeengeera peters out below a small cliff right underneath the Tooth. To gain the valley head you must now tend to the higher ground on your left. After twenty minutes and 200 feet you are in the 'The Pocket'. Its name is somewhat confusing,

A waterfall at the head of the Pocket

for the local people mean by 'The Pocket' the head of Glanmore Valley. A mile away and below you is the tumbledown shack mentioned by Healy and Windser. I remember a hermit who lived here. He frightened us when we were children.

The head of the pocket is a frightening enough place in any event, with its oily waterfalls and black cliffs disappearing into the mist. Puxley walked along its rim 200 years ago, and saw an Irish rebel army training by moonlight 2,000 feet below him. But the blackest deeds were done in this dark valley around a hundred years ago, for in that tumbledown shack lived Sean an Rabach.

One winter's night a British sailor climbed down out of the mist. In those days there was a British fleet at Castletown, and the man was probably a deserter. He asked the Rabach for lodging, and the Rabach responded by murdering him and burying him under his hearthstone in the early morning. A woman who was on her way to draw water happened to see the deed through the window. She kept silence for a while, but later lost her temper with the Rabach and told him that she knew something that would 'put him away for good'. And so the Rabach followed her up the cliff as she went to tend her cows and strangled her with a spancel (a rope for hobbling animals). He stuck her head down in a stream to simulate drowning.

Unfortunately for the Rabach that murder was witnessed too, by a man further up the hill stealing cows' tails. The Rabach was pursued, but hid in a cave in the rocks and so avoided capture.[7] His refuge is still known as Pluais an Rabach. It is about 200 feet above the shack in a steep gully to the west of it. The Rabach could outpace any policeman, for it is said that he had a double heart. It was the murdered woman's son who finally organised his capture, twenty years later. He told the police that the Rabach would be at home on Christmas night, and they surrounded his house. And so the Rabach was captured and hanged – the last man to meet his death this way in Munster, so they say.

4. Beara between the Healy Pass and the Kenmare–Glengariff Road

The county bounds follow the main ridge over Knockowen and Baurearagh to Turner's Rock on the T65. There is much high ground to the south of it. It is too rocky to be called a plateau and contains the fifty or so lovely Caha lakes. It ends in the southern spur of Sugarloaf.

Another ridge starts north of the county bounds at Coomnadiha. This swings north-east for eight miles and ends at Mucksna, just above Kenmare. From that Kenmare ridge one subsidiary ridge runs north-west for three miles from Knocknagorraveala, and another from Coomnadiha for six miles to Knockatee. Coums cut into this massif from all directions. From the west run little Glantrasna and the larger Glanrastel. From the north go Clonee, with five paternoster lakes, and Dromochty. The Baurearagh River cuts out another coum to the east, dividing the county bounds ridge from the Kenmare ridge. South of the Baurearagh are the Glengarrif and Coomarkane valleys. Finally there is Adrigole Valley to the south-west.

A fine five and a half hours can be spent on what I call the Big Horseshoe, though it is not a horseshoe in the proper sense as the start and finish are five miles distant. I start on the Carriganine Pass, which is between Knockanouganish and Knockreagh, on the L62, and finish at the top of the Healy Pass. The distance is eleven miles, giving an average speed of two mph in contrast to the one mph of the Cummeengeera horseshoe. The going is a lot easier. There is a hairpin bend on top of the Carriganine and just south of it a turf-cutter's road heads up the shoulder of Knockgarriff (1,459 ft). This road will take you half a mile up the hill. When you leave it you will see the advantage of the high start. You are already above the gorse, bracken and couch grass that make the start of so many Kerry walks unpleasant.

I sometimes divert north to Knockagarrane, which overlooks the tiny lough Napeasta. The direct route lies eastward over Knock-reagh and there follows a rather featureless trip up sloping bog to Coomnadiha: monotonous to the point that my son Ned calls this hill Coomnatedium. As you leave Coomnadiha you could be on the surface of the moon. This is a peneplain, an area where the bog burst is so extensive that little turf remains. You traverse shallow craters dotted with turf hags. Some of them look quite human. Ahead to your right is Knockowen. It looks near; but it will take three hours to reach it. For the present the going is over springy shale and very pleasant – quite often we run this bit.

I've spent a while trying to find the true summits of Caha and Eagles' Nest, both marked on the map as peaks of over 2,000 feet.

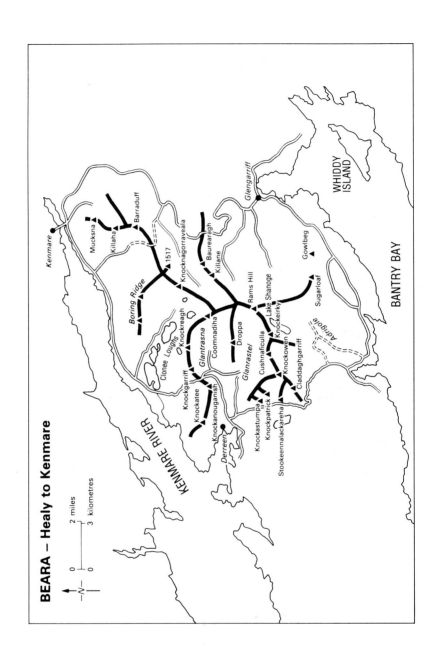

BEARA – Healy to Kenmare

They do not exist. Nor, really, do trig. point 1,941 or Ram's Hill. The next proper summit is Knockeirky. To reach it you descend to the head of Glanrastel, which is always wet. From that col you can see Lough Shanoge. This is one of the larger Caha lakes and it is alive with brown trout. Lord Bantry stocked these lakes 100 years ago.

The going now changes altogether. You are off the peneplain and on to rocky pavement and staircase. It is work interesting enough to let you forget the sweat of ascent. Knockeirky (1,906 ft) has a cairn, and so does Cushnaficulla beyond it, which has two summits. It is worth going over to the Northern one and peering into the depths of Glanrastel, now 1,500 feet vertically below you. Cushnaficulla, indeed, has a magnificent north face that is the steepest in Beara. It can be seen best from the floor of the valley.

On, then, to the tiny Lough Namimna, where I usually have lunch and a swim. There's a good natural diving board. But even on the hottest summer day the water has no more than a veneer of warmth in its top six inches. Below that it is very cold, always. Namimna is, after all, 2,000 feet up. From the lough there is a fine view north to the Matterhorn of Ireland – Mullaghanattin, across the Kenmare River.

It is three hundred feet to the top of Knockowen. Once again the going is rocky and interesting. Knockowen is a narrow wedge of a mountain whose top is a pointed rock which it is quite hard to balance on, so there have been very few true ascents of it.

Now you gaze westward to the great wall of Hungry Hill, then back east to Coomnadiha, perhaps shimmering in a heat haze, more often clothed in mist. The route on is downhill all the way over the several peaks of Claddaghgarriff, each one cairned. It is another two miles, but eventually you drop down to the tar of the Healy and perhaps buy a Coke from Don, who has a shop by the shrine. He's open in the summer holidays, except when the mist is down. In term time he drives the school bus.

As you travel north down the Healy you will see three smaller peaks rising to the right: Stookeenalakareha, Knockpatrick (not marked on the map) and Knockastumpa. These give a good low-level traverse of two hours or so on a bad day. Knockastumpa I call the hangover hill, for it is steep enough to sweat out the worst excesses. Often have I tackled it feeling no better than a warmed up corpse, and only just come to the conclusion that life may be worth while after all as I neared its top. From there goes a pleasant

The entrance to Glanrastel: Cushnaficulla on the left, the slopes of Knockowen on the right

enough traverse up the shoulder of Knockowen. This becomes particularly fine when you gain the lip of Glanowen, which is a small hanging valley above Glanrastel. And its good to come down over Stookeen, or perhaps Cladaghgariff.

The entrance to Glanrastel itself starts on the small road that branches east from the Healy a half mile south of the An Sibin pub. Alternatively, a road branches south off the Carriganine and then divides, its left hand branch taking you to Glantrasna and its right hand to Glanrastel. Glanrastel is an 'S' shaped valley all of five miles long. Leaving your car at the last farmhouse on the road from the Healy you round the shoulder of Knockastumpa along a boreen. You pass two deserted farmhouses and a massive boulder with a sheep-pen carved out beneath it. Below is the river, a turbulent burn with many a cascade, but many a rock-pool too which gives excellent swimming. You pass under the blanket cliffs, high on your right, and after a mile swing left and the full majesty of the Glen lies before you. The great cliffs of Cushnaficulla turn its south side into a veritable wall.

Directly above now is Glanowen. There's a good route up an obvious grass rake on the north face of Knockowen itself. It is particularly fine under snow, which lingers here in winter as the face receives no sun. But there must be other routes here that I have not tried. There is, for instance, a huge chimney going straight up the cliff; and there is also North Top, across the hanging valley from Knockowen's main summit. The reason, perhaps, why I have not been more adventurous hereabouts is that I had another rather memorable adventure here with my brother David in the early days.

Our goal was Cushnaficulla, which we had never climbed. There is a way up between its own cliffs and those of Knockowen, so off we set in our tweeds and brown shoes. We were on the summit in an hour. Thence another summit beckoned – Knockeirky – so we bagged two peaks for the price of one. On Knockeirky's summit we wondered what was the point now of going back over Cushnaficulla? Glanrastel was right below us. We looked over the edge and saw a pleasant series of grass terraces, beneath which there was nothing, just the valley floor 1,000 feet below. Not realising that a view of nothing is a bad view we slithered down the terraces. Soon we were forced to jump on to them; and each jump became longer than the last and each ledge smaller. In twenty minutes we were sitting on a grass tussock four feet square surrounded by slimy rock. Though we did not know it, we were a quarter of the way down the most vicious cliff in Beara.

Now we had to jump on to another tussock; our biggest jump yet. I threw my stick down ahead of me. Its impact on that tussock was considerable – the whole thing peeled off the cliff and disappeared. No sound except hissing, then, what seemed like a minute later, a massive crump and we saw our tussock and assorted rocks splaying out on the valley floor. The crump echoed round Glanrastel. Three times it came back to us, fainter but more prolonged, like thunder.

I told David that we must traverse. We edged our way along a narrow vegetable ledge to the west. Water was seeping over a

The Cushnaficulla cliff in Glanrastel

black overhang. The ledge petered out. We would have to go back. As we looked at the thin caterpillar of grass we had just crossed we realised that there was nothing supporting it from below. Inching back across the caterpillar, digging my shaking hands into the repulsive grey moss of the cliff above it, I regained the tussock and shouted to David to follow. But he got stuck in the middle of it. Crouching limpet-like, with his legs starting to shake, he shouted 'I can't make it'. 'Hold out your stick!' I yelled. He did so and I pulled him back to temporary safety.

We sat on that tussock for twenty minutes. Fear had led to indecision and fatigue; but we had to do something, for no one knew where we were. No strong man was going to materialise to rescue us. The only possible escape route was up again. What took twenty minutes to descend took an hour to scrabble back up. Vegetable footholds collapsed. Rock crumbled. Several times we slipped, but by some miracle we did not peel off the cliff. Eventually we regained its crest and collapsed quite exhausted. What next?

We headed east, towards the head of Glanrastel. Sometimes we climbed down a bit into the valley; but the greasy cliff still barred our descent, so we hauled ourselves back up again. We carried on thus for an hour or more. Suddenly, the Spirits of the Valley were kind to us. They showed us a grass rake leading diagonally down to the valley floor and bisecting the cliff, so we scrambled down and found ourselves in an unknown valley. (It was in fact the highest of Glanrastel's four basins, which we had never explored.)

Tired and depressed, we took two hours to limp back along the valley floor. It was dusk when we recovered our bicycles.

That was in August 1949. We felt that we had been saved by the ghosts of the valley, and even today as I walk up it I have the feeling that there are people watching us. These are surely the spirits of the people who scratched a living here before the Great Famine. A very charming people they must have been, for they seem to be watching in such a kindly way. They are gentle ghosts wishing us a safe journey through their valley.

I have talked to local people who all agree that this valley is haunted. Certainly it is steeped in history. South-east of Cummeenbaun is Pluais Carraig na Scriob, the 'den of the rock of the writings'. A slab of rock leans against another to form a den and the upright wall is inscribed over its full length. This could be the work of the Corco Duibne people in the fourth century, who developed their own alphabet called Ogam. Historians can now decipher it. Barrington gives the Roman equivalent of each letter in his *Discovering Kerry*.[1] 'Usually', he says 'the inscriptions are anything but eloquent. They are austere and uncommunicative, mainly names on gravestones, often giving also the descent of the deceased'. Often the descent from the pagan goddess Dovvinias has been obliterated and a Christian cross superimposed, presumably to 'convert' the stones and Christianise their power. But no one has yet deciphered the writing here in Pluais Carraig na Scriob. It could be that it is not Ogam at all but lines gouged out by the bayonets of the Whiteboys, a rebel army who hid here in the 1760s. In the nineteenth century the 'Invincible Number One' also hid here. He had been involved in the Phoenix Park murders of 1882 and eventually escaped by boat from Bantry to America.

As you proceed up the valley you come to Fionn Mac Cumhail's Step, a cliff twenty foot high and 500 yards long which reaches right across the valley floor. Fionn was a giant and perhaps his most spectacular feat was to scoop out a handful of earth, which became lough Neagh, and throw it over his shoulder into the Irish sea where it formed the Isle of Man.

Further up, the valley narrows to a chasm and you're forced to scramble along the south side of the river. But then it opens out again into another basin as large as the first. The river forms a string of natural swimming pools and it is therefore possible to swim in complete privacy. Each person in your party has his personal pool. Twice more the valley walls close in on you, and twice more they open out. In the highest basin of all there must be twenty waterfalls emptying the Caha lakes into the river.

Glanrastel is the most magical valley in Beara, which is saying a lot. It makes a good walk on a thick day, though the long grass of its upper reaches becomes quite sodden. There are many bogs, so you must expect to get thoroughly wet from the waist down, but it's worth it.

You eventually reach the head of the valley, which is the low point near Lough Shanoge that you will have gone over if you have done the big horseshoe. Indeed Shanoge seems to be a grand junction of the routes hereabouts. You can continue past it due south for a mile and plunge into the wild Adrigole Valley. This has

Glanrastel: the river meandering through the lower basin

a rare feature: a line of southward-facing cliffs which are not marked on the map. However if you find and follow the stream flowing from Lough Moredoolig you'll be able to climb down alright by following its true left bank, and then tending a little further east when you reach the steep ground.

Another route I've done that includes Shanoge is the very fine Sugarloaf Traverse. If you look at Sugarloaf from Glengarriff it is almost an aiguille, but in reality it's another whaleback like Knockowen, and you can get up it easily enough from the small road that loops north from the L61 at Derreenacarrin. It's only half an hour to the top, unless you wish to include a bit of a rock scramble. But from the top westwards over trig. points 1,871 and 1,776 is as tough as anything in Beara. Many a cliff and gully bar

Sugarloaf from Glengariff

your progress, and as you swing north the Caha lakes force you into more extensive diversions.

It is a bit dull to head due north to Glenlough Mountain: better to head for Moredoolig. That way you traverse a windswept plateau of tumbled boulders and glacis. This must be the wildest part of Beara. The last time we did this traverse was on a scorching August day. We plunged into Moredoolig and quenched our thirst as we swam through its blue waters, then we pressed on over Knock-eirky and Cushnaficulla. By the time we'd reached Namimna we were streaming with sweat again, so we had our second bathe and drink. The entry in our climbing book then reads 'Gasping over Knockowen we sank down gratefully to Don's cabin and an ice cold Fanta. Time, 7¼ hours of which no more than 5½ was walking!'

You'll also traverse Shanoge if you walk from the Healy to Kenmare. This trip is some sixteen miles and eight hours. Take the normal way up over Claddaghgarriff, Knockowen, Shanoge, Ram's Hill and trig. point 1,941. The County Bounds ridge runs north-west now, and you could be at the tunnel over the Kenmare–Glengarriff road in three miles. I've never been this way, as it lands you in the middle of nowhere and Sean O'Sulleabhain[7] describes it as full of ups and downs. Instead you continue north for a good mile and then dip off the peneplain on to a quite extraordinary sheet of rocky pavement that takes you down to the head of Clonee Valley. The pavement is like a giant lattice window. Veins of quartz criss-cross the sandstone to form a diamond pattern. At its bottom there is a small lake with a sharp grassy buttress behind it. That reaches out from Knocknagorraveala, which means, 'the hill of the midges'. If you have lunch by the lake you'll see why.

It's a boring haul up Knocknagorraveala, though the view eastward over the six lakes of Clonee is special. Once back on the crest your route continues north-west for two miles over another grassy summit. To your south the Forestry Commission have planted from the floor of the Baurearagh valley right up to the watershed. Above 1,250 feet the trees are hardly growing at all. They are small and gnarled and look like Japanese bonsais. Keeping these woods on your right you descend to the head of Dromochty Valley. On the map you will see a double line of cliffs marked; but this is fiction. It is a gentle slope with a few boulders.

The Dromochty col is 774 feet and you cross a tarred road which joins the Castletown and Glengarriff roads. Ahead now is more gentle country. The hills of the Barraduff circuit are rolling and clad in long heather. And so you sweat up Castle Rock and Barraduff. Now a sheep fence stretches along the ridge, but beware of sticking close to it, for lying in the heather are rusty wires from earlier fences. These foul your boots, or, worse, whip up and smack you smartly on the nose.

The route looks flat on the map, but there are many 50 and 100 foot hillocks on it, and the going is quite slow, particularly because you have already had a fairly arduous twelve mile walk and may be feeling the pace. But once on Killaha (1,569 ft) your problems are over. You look down on the neat triangle of Kenmare and its bridge over the estuary. On you go over Mucksna, the hill of the pigs, and down most easily south-east to the Barraduff valley.

Clonee Valley

Other routes off Mucksna have an excess of bracken and gorse hiding broken ground.

Now it's only half an hour to Kenmare and its thirty seven bars. You have a good walk behind you, though I must confess it is not my favourite, as everything east of Coomnadiha is a little tame.

Before leaving this central Caha massif I must track west again and mention two valleys and one spur that are all worth a visit.

The Clonee valley cuts in for four miles just north of Coomnadiha. To its north a thoroughly boring shoulder descends from Knocknagorraveala. Its main function seems to be blocking off the splendid view of the western Cahas. But Clonee Valley floor is most beautiful as it is virtually one long lake. In reality there are three lakes called Clonee, then a large lake, Inchiquin, then high above that Cummeenadillure and Cummeenaloghan. From that

Ishaghbuderlick

47

last one pours the stately Ishaghbuderlick waterfall, tumbling over another unmarked cliff. The Forestry Commission have planted much of this area with conifers, but to the south of Inchiquin there is a fine oak wood. Above that there's a cliff and another robber's den. This den is quite hard to find, and the final traverse into it lies across a slippery forty five degree slab. All that is known of the robber is that he was chased and killed on the Bunane side of the hills. In the chase he is said to have dropped a golden boot into the Inchiquin river.

It is good to climb on past the den to the summit of Eskana (called Cummeenanimna on the map) thence interestingly to Coomnadiha and down it again by the unique Rossard buttress between the two high lakes. Typically, the eastern ascent of Coomnadiha is far superior to the western. Even so, when you look behind you at the end of the day and say 'That's what I've just climbed' the 'That' is no more than a small pimple rising from the high plateau.

South of Coomnadiha is another fine valley; Glanrastel's other branch called Glantrasna. You gain it by leaving the L62 at the shrine on Knockanouganish, and you must keep left. The valley is short and ends abruptly at the cliff of Droppa. From it you can slog up Coomnadiha, which I do not recommend, or you can scramble up Droppa itself by a grass neck to the west of the cliff. This is steep. Then there's a pleasant ridge walk to the summit; and you can double back along the ridge to Cummeenbaun and then drop down to the little Pookeen (1,097 ft) whence there is a good traverse line to the even smaller Derreenataggart (994 ft) and so back to the valley.

Coomnadiha's western spur continues seaward of the L62. There are two rocky hills of just over a thousand feet: Knock-anouganish and Knockatee. The traverse of both takes only two hours.

Knockatee is very much our home mountain. Though its height is modest, its shape is satisfying. It is almost a perfect pyramid. The name means 'the house mountain' and it does indeed look like a house roof – even to the point that it has a minor summit as a chimney. It is a very easy climb and I do recommend it for all the family, whatever their age. The youngest child to climb it that I know of was Kate Bingham, aged three and a half.

The route is obvious from the top of the Knockatee road. The only feature is the great gully below the summit pyramid at

Knockatee

three-quarter height. The pyramid itself needs a bit of hand work. The top is small and gives a view over Kilmakilloge Harbour that is unbeatable. For those slightly more adventurous, its south ridge gives a bit of a scramble. Knockatee is an all-weather mountain for all comers. Even in rain, gale, snow or fog it is completely safe for toddlers or geriatrics.

5. Beara to the East of the Glengarriff Road

The two inlets that bound Beara come to an end at Kenmare and Bantry. Eastwards of a north–south line joining those two points Beara ceases, at least as a peninsula. And a change comes over the

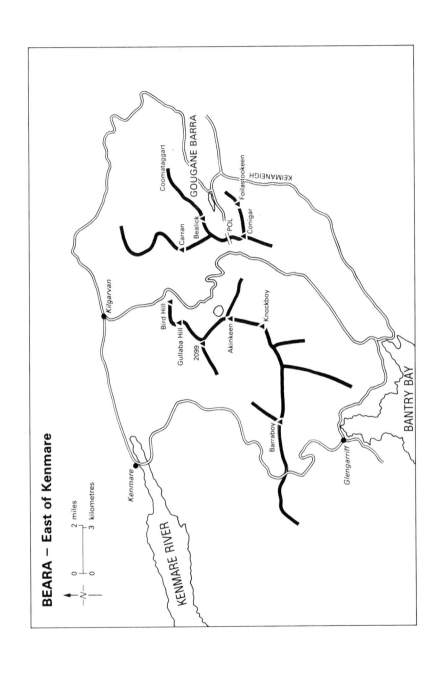

BEARA – East of Kenmare

N

0   2 miles

0   3 kilometres

KENMARE RIVER

Kenmare

Kilgarvan

GOUGANE BARRA

Coomataggart

Carran

Bealick

POL

Conigar

Foilastookeen

KEIMANEIGH

Bird Hill

Gullaba Hill

2099

Akinkeen

Knockboy

Barraboy

Glengarriff

BANTRY BAY

hills. Though Knockboy, at 2,321 feet, is higher than anything to its west, it is also gentler and duller. Fortunately there is still the odd coum hereabouts to add interest.

The County Bounds ridge continues eastwards from Turner's Rock over Esk and Barraboy mountains to a high motorable road marked very prominently on the map 'Priest's Leap'. The first time I came here I expected to find a spectacular cliff; but there's only a small flat rock. On it, so they say, a priest was surprised saying mass in penal times by English soldiers. He jumped on to his horse and made the ten miles to Bantry in a single leap. At Bantry you can see hoof marks on the rock where he landed, and even the mark of the whip that fell from his hand.

I trudged up Knockboy from the Priest's Leap. It was boring enough, but I wanted to conquer the highest peak in Beara; and peak bagging must be the only motive for anyone wishing to make this trip.

Just to Knockboy's north though, there's a good traverse over Akinkeen. I quote from our record of walks:

> From the top of the road between Kilgarvan and Glengariff we climbed Kinkeen (1,636 ft) and Akinkeen (2,280 ft), thence north to a shoulder, a trig. point at 2,099 ft, over a hill of around 2,050ft, Gullaba Hill (1,968 ft) and Bird Hill (1,339 ft). We went down to the school marked on the map, which is no longer a school, by the Slaheny river. Four and three-quarter hours.

The dramatic shape of that walk lay in lough Akinkeen and the considerable cliff above it. It was good to traverse its edge. After that my main memory is that the further you go inland, the taller the heather grows. Down Bird Hill it is thigh high.

East of that Kilgarvan–Glengarriff pass rises the small range of the Shehy mountains. The steep gorge of Keimaneigh cuts through them. Fork left at its northern end and you reach Gougane Barra. This is the south-eastern extremity of the Kerry/Cork hills, and the Forest and Wildlife Service have made it a tourist attraction.

The cliffs of Gougane Barra are most dramatic and a favourite subject for Victorian engravers. The traverse round Coomroe over Foilastookeen and Bealick gives a splendid trip of four to five hours. You climb up Foilastookeen from Gougane Barra chapel and you will soon see, to your north across the coum, Faill Dubh (The Black Cliff). The top of Foilastookeen is rather indefinite: there are a number of false summits. Continue west down to a saddle and up the 1,828 ft Maoloch. This is reputed to be the last nesting place in Ireland of the golden eagle.

Go on north-west and down to the sharp col of Poll (hole) through which runs a precipitous path which the pilgrims used to take from the Borlin valley on the west and on to Bealick (1,764 ft), which is an awkward cross-bench journey. On your left now is the Roughty valley. The Kenmare people used this as a route on Gougane Sunday, the last Sunday in September when they gathered to honour St Finbarr. A small cairn marks the top of Bealick. Now keep on the ridge east-north-east past a small lake, keeping the long line of cliffs on your right. When you reach the most easterly point of cliff, called Sron (nose), you can scramble down by the true left bank of the Owennashrone River, thence round the lake to the chapel. This is a holy valley. It was also the first resting place of the O'Sullivan Beare as he fled north in the seventeenth century.

Donal O'Sullivan Beare defended Dunboy Castle, near Bere Island, for nearly a year against the English. But in June of 1602 the English battered it to pieces. A great slaughter followed, and Donal gathered a thousand of his clan together to escape to Ulster. They started on Christmas Day, 1602, from Glengarriff.

Men, women and children, with neither food nor clothes, made for the wild lands of Gougane Barra. Some say they came by Keimaneigh, others that they climbed the steep pass into Coomroe. Either way it was a grim beginning to a terrible journey. All the way to Ulster they were dogged by enemies, cold, wet, and hunger. Of the 1,000 who set out only thirty-four men and one ageing woman reached the friendly territory of the O'Rourke's in Leitrim. Donal went on to Spain, where Philip III made him Count of Dunboy. Seventeen years later Donal, first Count of Dunboy, was killed in a brawl with his Irish valet!

Glanmore Lake and Foilemon

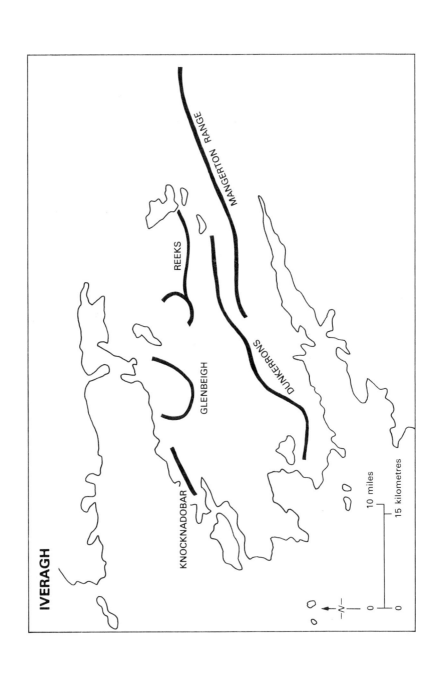

IVERAGH

MANGERTON RANGE

REEKS

DUNKERRONS

GLENBEIGH

KNOCKNADOBAR

10 miles

15 kilometres

N

0

0

Iveragh

Iveragh is the biggest of the three peninsulas and has the highest mountains. It is thirty miles long – the same as Beara – but double Beara's width. Iveragh is twenty miles north to south. You need all three half-inch maps of South Kerry to cover the peninsula. Numbers 20 and 21 have a good overlap, so there's no problem of walking over a map junction. But sheets 20 and 24 have no overlap at all and this can be awkward on the peaks west of Sneem. One blustery day I was walking south from Knocknagantee to Coomcallee. Lining up maps in driving rain is difficult and they tear quickly. Soon I gave up as it seemed obvious where Coomcallee rose. But I was wrong. The hill I climbed was the 1,950 ft Slievenashaska.

The topography of Iveragh is complicated. With both Beara and Dingle you're not far wrong if you describe them as each having one ridge running up the centre. But Iveragh presents you with a great jumble of peaks. It takes a while to sort them into separate ranges. I will try to do so, starting in the south-west corner.

Here lie the Dunkerrons. The first peak is the little cliff of Reenearagh, at Hog's head; then come the higher tops of Mullaghbeg and Eagle's Hill. The range tends northward now over Coomcallee, where it breaks the 2,000 foot contour, on over Knocknagantee, Coomnacronia, Fineraragh, Beounn, and Mullaghanattin – 2,539 feet and Kerry's finest peak. The Ballaghbeama pass now cuts through the range, which continues east over the large but unlovely Knockduff (2,571 ft), then tends lower at Knocknabreeda and finally fizzles out in the Black Valley.

The Dunkerrons are twenty one miles long as the crow flies, but more like forty as the man walks. The Ballaghbeama gap is a good reference point in Iveragh, as two other ranges start here. Three

The Iveragh peninsula stretching westward from the Reeks

miles south-east of it Knocklomena marks the start of the Mangerton range. That goes over Boughill, Peakeen, Mangerton itself,
Stoompa and Crohane and stretches twenty three miles, again as
the crow flies. The Paps are in the same line but are really part of
the Derrynasaggarts.

The MacGillycuddy Reeks start four miles north-west of the
Ballaghbeama. They rise to Curraghmore, Caher, and Carrauntoohill, at 3,414 feet the highest peak in Ireland. They continue at
over 3,000 feet along the ridge of the Reeks before the extraordinary Gap of Dunloe slices through. Then they rise up again more
gently over Purple Mountain and Tomies before tumbling into
Killarney's lower lake.

The Reeks are only thirteen miles long. Many a tourist calls all Iveragh mountains 'The Reeks', but he is wrong. The real Reeks are a short, sharp, isolated cluster north of the two long ranges (Dunkerron and Mangerton) that form the true backbone of Iveragh.

West and a bit north of the Reeks is the Glenbeigh Horseshoe, a fourteen mile circuit, and west of that rises the separate five mile massif of Knocknadobar. There's a lower horseshoe south of Cahirciveen and many another isolated hill of 1,500 feet or so dotted around the peninsula.

That is about as simple as I can make Iveragh. There are sixty three tops of over 2,000 feet compared to Beara's nine. There are six over 3,000 compared to Beara's nil. There must be fifty coums, and 200 lakes. And the peninsula does not divide up neatly north–south as Beara does. The best way to describe its hills, I think, is to take them one range at a time, even if that range is crossed by a road.

I said that the southernmost range, the Dunkerrons, started at Hog's Head. But with imagination I think of them as continuing west even of that: under the sea they go, rearing out of it again at Deenish and Scariff Islands. Therefore I will start this section with descriptions of Iveragh's western isles and rocks, just as I did with Beara.

1. Iveragh's Islands

You approach Scariff by boat from West Cove. It is uninhabited and cliff-bound, though there is a fair landing-place with steps cut out of the living rock. Of course you should only attempt this on a calm day. You will notice remains both Pagan and Christian. Here in the fourteenth century there was a terrible drowning of Cornish nuns.

Sir John Arundel, a knight of Cornwall, recruited a band of wild youths and raided a convent near Penzance. They carried the nuns to their ship, where followed scenes of 'unrestrained and frightful debauchery'.[1] They sailed on to Ireland and when they were off Scariff a great gale arose. To placate the 'demon of the storm' they threw the nuns into the Atlantic. All the nuns died and Arundel's ship was smashed against Scariff's cliffs. Sir John scrambled ashore, only to be hauled back to his death by an enormous wave.

Later, Lord Lansdowne's agent, W.S. Trench, swam into one of Scariff's great caves to hunt seals. His party swam with spears and wore peculiar caps with candles sunk into them to illuminate the quarry.

The only regular Scariff visitor whom I know of today is Lord Waterford. He and his sons are dropped on it each year for a week or two without food. They take guns and live off rabbits, seals and seagulls.

There is a keen tide race between Scariff and Deenish Island which has a beach. In truth I have never landed on either, but I have been to Great Skellig to the north. There are regular services to the Skelligs from Portmagee, Reenard, Cahirciveen and Derrynane. I went from Portmagee, crammed into a small boat along with some forty other souls – quite a dangerous load should a storm blow up. However, it kept calm for the twelve mile trip and we saw in the oily smooth waters rafts of Manx Sheerwaters and a lazy blue shark. Two parts of the blue shark stick out of the water. Behind the triangular dorsal fin was a great half-crescent of tail. The boatman told us that he was harmless, though I have read otherwise.

We sailed close under the Little Skellig, where there is one of the largest gannet colonies off Ireland – 20,000 pairs nest here. The rock is most precipitous and it is hard to spot a landing point. Our boatman told us that no one had ever landed there and got off the island alive.

A mile and a half on is Great Skellig, or Skellig Michael. The landing here is a lot easier than that on to the Bull. It's an easy walk up a broad path to the lighthouse, and half way along that path the old steps to the monastery climb right to the top of the ridge. Should you be unable to land in the normal place, which is called Blind Man's Cove, there are other rougher landing places at Cross Cove and Blue Cove. Whatever the wind direction, one of these three will be in the lee. From Cross Cove you are winched up by derrick.

Skellig Michael has a long religious history: first pagan, then monastic, then of pilgrimage. Before the fifth century the people here worshipped serpents but then St Patrick arrived. Indeed this is the only part of Kerry that he did visit, contrary to what they tell you in Killarney. St Patrick climbed the rock and 'held his arms aloft in prayer like Moses'[1] He fought the 'evil things and venomous serpents' with the help of St Michael and All Angels. The

58

serpents were driven to the top and over 700 feet of sheer cliff to perish in the sea.

The beehive huts that stand on top of Skellig are *clochans*: – the oldest form of dwelling known to man. For six hundred years monks lived up here. Their lifestyle was austere and unchanging. How beautiful it must have been on the fine mild days; but how terrifying in the Atlantic storms. Recently one wave damaged a lighthouse 175 feet up the cliff face. Probably the Skellig monastery was one of a pair; the other at Balinskelligs, on the mainland, could have been its supply depot. Skellig was the 'ultimate practicable retreat from the world', in Barrington's[1] words. 'It gave a taste of that paradisal place that lay beyond the ocean and inspired St Brendan to voyage to the Western World.'

The monastery was abandoned around 1300, and then the pilgrimages started. They only ended in 1850 when 'Pilgrims came to Skellig for Holy Week and bad behaviour forced the police to clear the rock.'[1] The pilgrims came for varied reasons: some because they were holy men; others as a penance for their wickedness. Thus a boat-load of monks was lost in Cross Cove, and at about the same time a murderer was ordered here from Armagh. Heneas Mac Hail was his name. He had killed his son, and his punishment was to visit all the Irish penitential stations – quite a lenient penalty for the period, really (1543).

There grew up, too, the curious practice of the Skellig Lists. Since the Skellig monks were never influenced by the Roman calendar they celebrated Easter some three weeks later than did the mainland, and their Lent started later too. Young lovers on the mainland who had jumped the gun were told to 'get married before Lent'. Their names were put on the list, and they were all shipped out to Skellig for shot-gun weddings. When I was on Skellig I forgot to ask the lighthouse keeper if he still kept the old Easter dates.

There is a col on top of the Skellig. To the east is the monastery, and Barrington in *Discovering Kerry*, has a very full account of that. To the west of the monastery is the penitential station, an arm of rock that overhangs the sea 700 feet below. I climbed towards it. The route is quite straightforward. At first there's a ledge all of a foot wide, then there are good footholds cut out of the rock. But the exposure is really terrific. I came to a steepish chimney and at that point I looked down at the sea. I thought of the serpents that had plunged to their deaths there. I thought too of the English

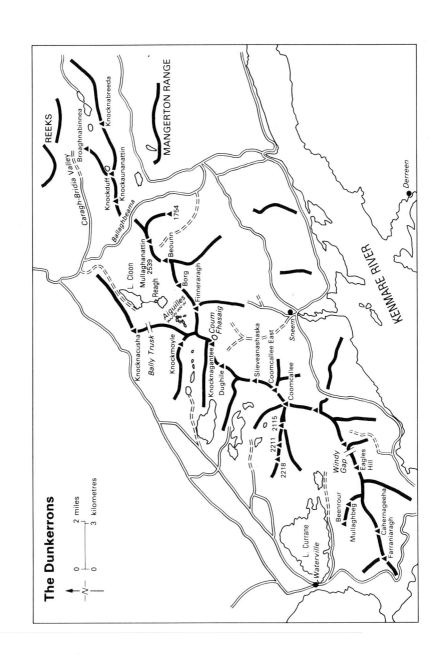

The Dunkerrons

N

0   2 miles

0   3 kilometres

REEKS

Caragh-Bridia Valley

Knockduff

Broaghnabinnea

Knocknabreeda

Knockaunanattin

MANGERTON RANGE

Ballaghbeama

Mullaghanattin 2539

L. Cloon

Reagh

Borg

Beoun

1754

Finneraragh

Aiguilles

Knocknacusha

Coum Fhasaig

Bally Trusk

Knockmoyle

Knocknagantee

Dughile

Slieveanashaska

Coomcallee East

Sneem

Coomcallee

2211

2115

2218

Windy Gap

Eagles Hill

Beenrour

Mullaghbeg

Cahernageeha

Farraniaragh

L. Currane

Waterville

KENMARE RIVER

Derreen

soldier who had mocked the devotions and who also fell to the sea, uttering the curiously pedestrian words, 'What a long way it is to fall.' Then my courage failed and I returned shakily to the col. So Skellig Michael is my only unconquered Kerry peak.

2. The Dunkerron Range

The pretty seaside resort of Waterville is the best centre for exploring the western summits of this long chain. After the Windy Gap, the Dunkerrons run north for some six miles, forming an 'L'. Within the 'L' are several loughs two miles long, like Derriana, and another second in size only to Killarney's lower lake. This is Lough Currane, seven square miles of water butting against the steep mountainside of Mullaghbeg to the south, and hemmed in to the east by Coomcallee.

Lough Currane holds many salmon, which must enter it by the half mile of river flowing into Ballinskelligs Bay. For that reason the river is a veritable salmon trap which you can hire by the half hour and still catch a couple of fish if you are sufficiently expert. There's a beautiful drive along its southern shore to another Glanmore Valley and the smaller Isknagahiny Lough above it. If you park by the school you can do a good circuit over Eagle's Hill and Mullaghbeg, starting up Windy Gap (only one of several so named in Kerry). A boreen is marked on the map here, but we could not find it until we reached the top of the col, and then it is obvious that you are better off it in any event, since it is built of rough ankle-twisting stones, whereas the hillside is of good springy turf.

It was the lambing season, and my wife took pity on a lamb and mother separated by cliff. She picked up the woolly bundle and, carrying it some way around the cliff, set it down beside the mother, who, unfortunately, showed no interest at all and so was clearly not the mother. The question then arose: which of the many bleating lambless sheep was the true mother? There must have been twenty of them scattered up to the top of the hill. My wife tried two more ewes before leaving the lamb on its own. The chances are that it died soon after. Such is nature. On other hills we have helped sheep that have become trapped in fences, or are on their backs unable to right themselves. But the failures stick in the mind. On Killaha we righted a sheep to find it had already lost its eyes to the crows. It would have been kinder to kill it.

61

Eagles Hill has a graceful sweep of a west shoulder, and a short steep east one: very typical. The 300 feet up from Windy Gap is the sort of slope that causes a man addicted to Afton Major to pause for breath every fifty steps or so. The top is very disappointing. It is a peneplain, with bog burst, and the trek over to Mullaghbeg is marred by many a risky jump into a muddy dyke.

On the col above Lough Coomrooanig starts 'the road to nowhere'. It is cut out of the bog, and follows the crest west to Cahernageeha and Carraniaragh. Conceivably it links up with the road running north from Caherdaniel, but we never found out, as we preferred exploring the cliffs of Mullaghbeg to the long trudge west which would end at the Ring of Kerry road at Coomakista Pass.

The way off the peneplain over Mullaghbeg is more dramatic. To go due north, indeed, would pound you on a cliff. But the cliff marked on the map to the east-north-east of Mullaghbeg does not exist. It's a thoroughly good descent and we looked down into the harsh corrie that holds the lake. We hit the road a couple of miles west of the car, and that trip took us four hours twenty minutes. This included a leisurely lunch break and, of course, the incident of the orphan lamb.

I've had a good winter circuit over the peaks to the north of Eagles' Hill. It lay round Loughs Iskanamakteery and Nambrackdedarrig, lakes which Barrington describes as 'attractive on a bright day, but memorable on a threatening one.'[1] An important feature hereabouts is that there are cliffs facing west; so the golden rule that it's always safe to go west in mist does not apply to the north–south section of the Dunkerrons.

It is seven years since I made this journey, so I think it best to quote from our journal:

> An initial difficulty in crossing the Cummeragh River. The roads marked across it simply ford it and it looked wide, deep, and cold. I eventually crossed by bridge on the road from Dromod and left the car at Oughtiv hamlet. Here I met a poor man living in a caravan who had a septic foot. He had been to Cahirciveen for treatment but it had had no effect. He asked for ointment but I could not help. Then with great courtesy he said he would mind my car while I travelled the hills.
>
> So I struck up the spur between Iskanamakteery and Cloonaghin lakes. I swung right to the fine peak of Slieveanashaska which gave a fine view of our home harbour, Kilmakilloge, across the Kenmare River. After the fine view there came cloud and snow. However, I pressed on to scale Coomcallee, whose top is

about as easy to find as Caha's in thick fog. The weather cleared. I swung west over the flattish peaks (2,115 ft, 2,211 ft, and 2,218 ft). The view of Lough Currane and the snowy summits of Eagles' Hill and Mullaghbeg beyond it was alpine. The last peak, 2,218 ft, turned into a good narrow ridge. Easily back to the car and the man with the septic foot, who had guarded it for five hours but refused any form of payment – even Afton Majors.

This central section of the Dunkerrons is massive but dull compared to the eastern (Mullaghanattin/Knockmoyle) section. It was too cold to stop for lunch: I had it in the car with the heater at full blast. Time five hours.

The Dunkerrons continue north after Coomcallee. Between it and Knocknagantee is an area wild and rocky with many a lake on the summit ridge, and deep coums cutting in from both sides. I do recommend a circuit here. If you turn north at the Market Cross in Sneem you can get right under Knocknagantee and swing west then south from it, ending over Slievenashaska. It's only a six mile trip but you'll do well to better one mile an hour. Knocknagantee itself is a fine hill. Most of its south face is one big friction slab giving a delicate ascent. Further east it plunges 900 feet to the lough in Coum Fhasaig. That corrie is surrounded by cliff on three sides. Joss Lynam has climbed Knocknagantee's east face by several routes, though that sort of slimy vegetable affair fills me only with trepidation.

Leaving Knocknagantee we swung over several unnamed peaks which I have called after features near them: we went south over Dughile (c 1,950 ft), trig. point 1,863, and finally Slievenashaska, named after the lake to its north. We had an all too common bit of trouble with the car that day: getting it bogged on the turn. The coum roads of Kerry get worse imperceptibly as you near their ends. Good tar changes slowly to tar with grassy strip in the middle. Then the tar runs out altogether and the dirt road narrows. Either side of it will be a ditch. Always, though, there is a farmyard at its end, and the knack is to spot the one piece of flat ground that is not bog. It helps to get out and jump around a bit.

I was with my son, but he was only ten and too small to push the car with me in it, steering and revving to reverse. So we changed roles. Ned had only driven a bicycle before, but he managed to reverse the car four feet with right hand hard down, then to slam on the brakes only one inch away from a sharp slab of rock. We were back on hard standing.

A little further north I did my most desolate walk one winter: that

Coum Fhasaig

was the circuit of Coomavoher. It is the most northerly of the four coums that cut into the massif from the west and contains six lakes, some little more than ponds. You approach it from the Waterville–Killorglin road, taking a small turn east that snakes up beneath the lowest lake, called Torreenbog.

Cloud was around a thousand feet. My first goal was Knockmoyle. This is quite a respectable looking peak from the north, but it is featureless bog from the south: no place to be in mist. I stuck to the valley floor as far as the third lake and then climbed very steeply up the cliff. As the mist closed in on me I have seldom felt more lonely. The trudge over the summit bog was, if anything, a bit worse, in fine sleet.

Back from the summit I travelled on a new bearing and became quite dispirited until I saw before me a sheet of water. It was the topmost of the six lakes. I was dead on course for Knocknagantee, and at the top of that there is a cairn. Then one of those magical changes happened to the weather which make the real glory of hill-walking in Kerry: suddenly, I had a view. It was straight down 1,000 feet to the lake in the floor of Coum Fhasaig. In another minute the cloud cleared the tops and I could see back to the little landmark lake on the col and the black summit of Knockmoyle beyond it. South I looked across the Kenmare River to the Cahas, basking in a wintry sun. I jogged back west along Coomavoher's south shoulder (there's not much cliff here, despite the map marking) and I was back at the car in four and three-quarter hours. If you're after the wildest walk in Kerry, this is it.

My next trip into Coum Fhasaig was with a large party in high summer. This was the traverse of the ridge from the Ballaghbeama Gap to the col just east of Knocknagantee. This trip needs a willing base camp driver to dump you at the pass and then travel to Sneem to pick you up. The walk took us seven and a half hours.

Ballaghbeama is a dramatic gorge topping out at 852 feet. The rainfall in Ballaghbeama is 130 inches. Surprisingly, no stream flows from it. Ballaghbeama means 'Pass of the Cut'. Perhaps it was cut by a short-lived torrent in the waning phase of the last ice age. Its floor is littered with boulders.

The route west up Knocknavulloge (1,505 ft) is very steep. I remember that we had just returned from climbing some Munroes of 3,800 and even 4,000 feet in Scotland, and that we looked on this lowly traverse as a bit of a rest cure. But by the time we had

Ballaghbeama. The route up Knocknavulloge

breasted Knocknavulloge to see Mullaghanattin 1,000 feet above us and nearly two miles away we had revised our view. Always take your hat off to a Kerry mountain.

We slogged up the 'Matterhorn of Ireland' which looks best from away to the north-west on another pass, the Ballaghisheen. It is steep enough in all conscience. The descent to its western col is even steeper and would surely be naked rock if it were on Beara. Beyond the col are two steps that look vertical until you come to them. Here lies a tablet in memory of a Dublin man, Noel Lynch. He was a climber of international repute who was killed on this 'straightforward' Kerry walk.

The next peak is a saddleback: Beounn, with the satisfying height of 2,468 feet. From a western point like Derryhane, Beounn

The flattest or 'Table Mountain' aspect of Beounn

is an aiguille, but from due south it's more like Table Mountain. It is a grand easy stroll along its heathery top and you scramble down then to the gap above Coum Lough. The peak towering beyond it marks the eastern end of a long ridge ending at Finneraragh. My first approach to that Coum Lough gap had been from the north on a black winter's day, when I reckoned that there was a *mauvais pas* blocking it from the ridge. The ascent looked quite vertical and, with cloud descending, I cried off. But that summer's day we had no difficulty in climbing the *mauvais pas*. It is only very steep grass and when we were on top we set up the chant '*two, four, six, eight, who do we appreciate* – Beounn (pronounced Bjorn) *Borg!*' And so we named the hill above the *mauvais pas* after the Swedish tennis champion.

As you gain 'Borg' and head west, the going becomes a lot rougher. The double line of cliff to both north and south on the map is genuine. There is no escape and you must press on to Finneraragh. This is a hill of naked rock. Walls and gullies alternate with acres of smooth slab. The top is disappointingly flat.

And west of Finneraragh it gets rougher still. We pressed on slowly to Coomnacronia (2,086 ft) and saw Coum Fhasaig for the first time from the west. From here Knocknagantee's cliffs glower down on you and Joss Lynam's conquest looks impressive indeed. A thin cascade tumbles down them, and a bigger one falls from the col to the north. Knocknagantee is only a mile away, but to reach it you must loop north around Coum Fhasaig, and that day we decided to give it a miss. Instead we tumbled and slithered to the floor of the coum. It was hot enough for a swim, but this is always quite a performance as climbing boots are not the quickest type of footwear to take off and put on again. So I settled for a half-swim for which the instructions are:

1. Remove shirt.
2. Find rock overhanging lake.
3. Plunge top half of body upside down into water holding nose.

I wish I could recommend this: but really it is most unpleasant and there's a big danger of toppling into the water altogether. One lives and learns.

After scrambling down from Fhasaig under the cliffs, we hit the road, and the only slightly boring section of this magnificent walk followed: a four mile trek to Sneem. However willing your base camp driver might be it is hard for him to go further than Sneem as

Knocknavulloge, Mullaghanattin, Beounn and Borg from the North

there are several roads up this valley and it would be bad news indeed if you chose the eastern road with your driver waiting at the top of the central one. So, though this route needs a bit of organisation it must rank amongst the finest in Kerry and is an essential part of any holiday.

There are other ways up and routes off Mullaghanattin. There's its 'pocket' to the south, which you reach by forking left four miles south of the Ballaghbeama. At the last farmhouse you simply walk up a grassy slope of increasing steepness to the summit. This is monotonous and ghastly. As you pant up the hillside that seemingly has no end remember a shepherd who climbed this way to watch his flock. One day he found a fox attacking his sheep at the summit, so he ran down to his cottage to get a rifle, ran up again, and shot the fox.

Beyond Lough Reagh, the aiguilles

Some say that this climb is a little less awful if you head east to the ridge above Bohacullia. But whichever route you take you are slogging up a western slope. Once on top, however, you can circuit easily over Beounn and then south to Derreenagreer (1,725 ft). The cliffs on the map are largely non-existent and the trip takes only three hours.

I've also come off Mullaghanattin by the obvious ridge due north, and thence back to the Ballaghbeama. Once I came off it north-east, but that is precipitous and not recommended. Sean O'Suilleabhain[7] recommends that you include it in the Cloon Horseshoe circuit: however that too involves complicated car work, and I prefer to drive as far as I can into that valley and go directly up Beounn. You drive up to the end of Lough Cloon, through three gates, and leave the car by a double cottage. Unfortunately Mullaghanattin is off route behind you and to include it would mean a three mile walk back along the road. The north-east spur of Beounn, though, is only a few hundred yards away.

On my first trip up here the weather was so bad that I did not even attempt Beounn. I preferred simply to walk up the valley, and it is fortunate that I did, for the end of it is as dramatic as anything in Kerry. It's a mile on to Lough Reagh. The going is wet and at one stage Beounn's cliffs plunge straight into the lough, so I trod warily. Beyond Reagh is the wood of diagonal oaks. These scrubby trees grow out of a thirty degree slope, but they clearly think that they are on flat ground, for they grow straight out of the slope, all leaning thirty degrees southward.

Beyond that amazing wood are the Lough Reagh Aiguilles, sharper than any other rock faces in Kerry. These are six pinnacles rising sheer from the valley floor. H.C. Hart, a member of the Alpine Club, wrote of them in 1895:

> They are a most superbly rugged cluster of sugar-loaf peaks huddled together and often separated by sheer precipices and inaccessible ravines. Many gullies of sound rock occur. Bad weather on two different visits rendered climbing here an unpleasant experience, but enough was seen to enable the writer to pronounce the district well worthy of a visit. Mount Aitchin (Whin Mount) is the chief summit.

The Federation of Irish Mountaineering Clubs have done some routes up them. Also Sean O'Suilleabhain mentions a steep gulley cutting through them which ends on flat slabs north of Coomalougha lake. The map, too, marks that route as cliff-free for walkers, but I have never done it. Dominating this valley to the north is the fine peak of *c.* 2,150 feet that I call Knockmoyle East.

Now for the Cloon Circuit.

Beounn's north spur is grass to half height. Then it gives a steep rocky scramble, the angle eases, and you have gained Beounn's ridge: a bit like Swirrel Edge on Hellvellyn. You swing over it and down to the col and the *mauvais pas*, just like the last walk. On likewise over Borg and Finneraragh. The mountain has a fine east face plunging down to the Corrie of Lough Coomeen.

Leave Finneraragh bearing north-east and you soon gain the

couch grass of the Knockmoyle declivity. On your right are the seven lakes that feed the torrent tumbling between Reagh's aiguilles. On your left you may just see the topmost of the six paternoster lakes of Coomavoher. The Reagh aiguilles look innocent enough from above. I had a quiet lunch by a stream in the declivity's bottom and then I trudged up Knockmoyle. This was boring and probably it would be better to go straight for Knockmoyle East. This, ironically, shows up the real Knockmoyle as a fine hill with a steep northern flank.

I went down to Ballytrusk and the going got rough and wet. From the col south of Ballytrusk I dropped down to the valley. I seemed to be walking on waterlogged sponge. As I reached that valley floor I consoled myself with the thought that I could not get any wetter: but I was wrong. The area between Cloon and Reagh is a marsh and I waded through it waist deep.

My walk took six and a half hours. I would say that there is not much of interest after you have left Finneraragh and therefore not much point to it if you have also done the Mullaghanattin/ Coomnacronia traverse. Perhaps it might be better to continue north from Ballytrusk to Knocknacusha, then descend to Canknoogheda. That would make a big day. And it would certainly make sense to search out Sean O'Suilleabhain's route through the aiguilles and then traverse south-east to Beounn. That could well be the most exciting route round Cloon.

At the Ballaghbeama you will have seen the Dunkerron range continuing eastward. That way is the highest point of the range: Knockduff, at 2,572 ft. The hill looks ungainly from a distance but gives very airy ridge-walking.

I have circuited Knockduff from the Bridia valley, the source of the Caragh River. You get there by turning right three miles north of the Ballaghbeama. And for comfort you need another willing driver, or a second car left at the top of the Ballaghbeama. In Bridia you are under the huge southern wall of Curraghmore (2,776 ft), the most southerly Reek. Thirty years ago I had just learnt to drive and I took David up here in an old banger of a van. We'd been aiming at the Reeks, but the cloud was low so we settled for Broaghnabinnea (2,440 ft). When we got back to the van the engine had seized solid, so we asked in the cottage if they knew of a mechanic. They told us of one a four mile cycle-ride away; so David and I tossed for who was to make the bike trip and he lost. Forty

From Curraghmore's shoulder looking West towards Mullaghanattin &
Beounn

five minutes later he was back with a charming fellow, who poked about in the van, mainly in the areas of the exhaust and the fuse box. For an hour or so he examined the patient before pronouncing it incurable. Then he gave us a lift to the mouth of Bridia and left us to walk over the Ballaghbeama. I had no money, but gave him four packets of Players.

I reckoned that we'd average four miles an hour and be in Kenmare by dusk. But we were both tired. A few miles north of the Blackwater estuary it grew dark and we settled down under a gorse bush to spend the night. That was in 1953. In those days there were no cars around. It started to rain so we tunnelled under the gorse for shelter, but we were pretty cold and hungry after a couple of hours. Then we saw to our amazement an old lorry on the Killarney–Sneem Road. We asked the driver most naively if he could take us to a taxi. He said, 'Sure, there's one only a few hundred yards away.' Of course it was not a taxi in the proper sense of the word, with a meter. It was a pre-war Ford, but it worked. We aimed for the Derreen Agent's house in Kenmare, for he, we hoped, would be able to pay our fare. He obliged and drove us towards Derreen. It was now 11 p.m. Five miles out of Kenmare we met two worried parents driving towards us. My mother asked if we were hurt. My father uttered the two memorable words 'Breakdown? *Exactly.*'

Today you may be charged for car-parking in Bridia. You are near the commercialism of Killarney, and its a sorry contrast to Coomavoher and my friend with the septic foot.

You can slog up Broaghnabinnea's west flank, but we walked on up the valley connecting Bridia to Cummeenduff, the famous Black Valley of Killarney. A path is marked on the map but it is indistinct.

At the col, around 950 feet, we struck up Broaghnabinnea's north side, which is steep and invigorating. There are rock ribs and a huge quantity of loose stones. Careful as we were, we dislodged some which hurtled down the mountain and soon we thought it safer to climb in line, abreast. The top of Broaghnabinnea is a boggy field with a fence across it; a real anti-climax after the alpine ascent. It will, however, give the first view of that great grey wall of the Reeks to the north.

It's a thousand easy feet down to Coumreagh. Normally this sort of descent is terrible for morale at the start of the day, but the ridge rising ahead to Knockduff is so spectacular that losing height does not seem to matter. It's a grand rocky scramble up it. Soon we were on a very narrow arête running due south and marked (correctly) by a double line of cliff on the map. Beneath us Lough Duff glinted ominously black.

Knockduff's ridges form a T-junction: that is why it looks so flat from a distance. When you get to the 'T' you can go east and follow the Dunkerrons to their rather tame end at Derryard. We went that way once, but the hills were unremarkable so we came off them too soon and had a perilous descent over Knocknabreeda's north cliff. There's a fine double cascade above Lough Reagh in Black Valley. You can walk up beside it and so on to Knockduff from the east. However, that's a diversion.

When we got to Knockduff's T-junction we turned right towards

Broaghnabinnea with the Reeks on its left

the Ballaghbeama. The route continued west in spectacular fashion. We crossed a hill of some 2,260 feet and then Knockaunanattin, with all the time a good cliff to our right. Thence over trig. point 1,532 and easily down to the Ballaghbeama. We took five and a half hours.

3. The Mangerton Range

You will have seen Knocklomena as you drove north to the Ballaghbeama Pass. It is an unlovely hummock and marks the western end of the Mangertons. Generally these mountains are less vicious than the Dunkerrons: there's less rock, more heather. The exception is an area of frantic volcanic activity between Mangerton and Crohane.

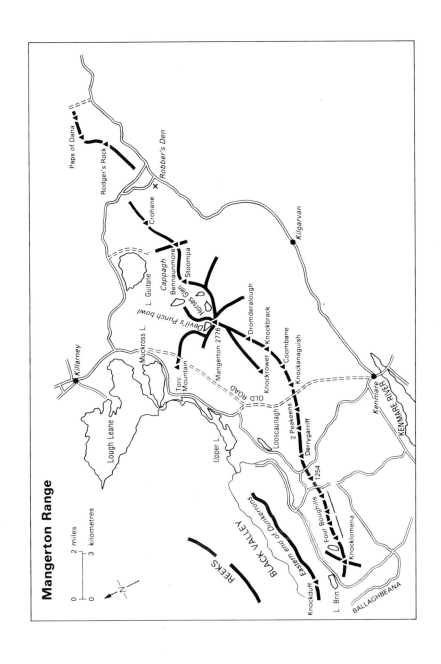

Mangerton Range

0   2 miles
0   3 kilometres

N

REEKS

BLACK VALLEY

Eastern end of Dunkerrons

Killarney

Lough Leane

Muckross L.

L. Guitane

Paps of Dana

Rodger's Rock

Crohane

Robber's Den

Kilgarvan

Cappagh

Bennaunmore

Stoompa

Holses Glen

Devil's Punch bowl

Dromderalough

Knockbrack

Mangerton 2776

Torc Mountain

Upper L.

Knockrower

Coombane

Knockanaguish

OLD ROAD

Looscaunagh

2 Peakeens

Derrygarriff

1254

Four Boughills

Knocklomena

L. Brin

Knockduff

BALLAGHBEANA

Kenmare

KENMARE RIVER

You can slog up Knocklomena from the Killarney–Blackwater road in twenty minutes if you like that sort of thing. There's not a lot you can do from its top as it is cut off to the east by the cleft of Lough Fadda. A finer lough, Brin, lies north-east. This is the source of the Blackwater, and it adds to the legend of Fionn MacCumhail, for it is named after his dog, Bran, who pursued a stag into the lake. Both drowned, but sometimes even today a great creature like a white greyhound has been seen on its shores. And a local cow gave birth to an animal that was half calf and half hound.

East of Knocklomena lies a small range of four peaks, only one of which is named: Boughill, pronounced Bookle, which means a standing rock. The rock is marked on the map. Its front gives a little scramble, and from there I've climbed to the top (2,065 ft) and traversed west over the three peaks. We call them 'The Four Boughills'.

It's a bad slog up Boughill, with many a false summit. It could be more exciting to climb up the cliff that rises from Lough Barfinny. Indeed if you look at Boughill from near Dinish, in Beara, that right-hand edge seems vertical. Whatever your route, the view from the top is particularly fine, and the ridge on to Boughills II and III is steep and rocky. It's easy then over grass to Boughill IV. From there you drop down and walk back two miles to the car. This is a rather gentle four hour trip.

For the next group of hills, Peakeen, you head north from Kenmare past the hospital and fork right. Leave your car at Gowlane Cross, and walk on along the old Kenmare–Killarney Road, which is no more than a dirt track and undriveable.

Peakeen (1,825ft) has a fine east face, which gives a mere 800 feet of ascent from the top of the pass. This pass, too, is called Windy Gap and there's a third so called in Dingle. We climbed up here once after a long drought. The inch of rain the night before had marked its end. I see from our journal that 'the hills had reverted to liquid form and their colour was back to those mystical shades of black, blue, grey and pink peculiar to Kerry'.

We traversed trig. points 1,774 and 1,728. Then we went on to Derrygarriff. From there it's quite satisfying, in a nasty sort of way, to gloat over the traffic below you choking up the Kenmare–Killarney Road. We looked down on that crooked route to see cars packed with children stuck behind buses, tractors and donkey-carts. Our morale was high; we were relaxed; but we knew that a few hundred feet below us frustrated drivers were trapped in their steel boxes with fidgety children behind them crying or feeling sick.

I have only just realised how dangerous it is to walk along a main road after a climb. It hit me when a furious motorist hit me in Glencoe. A man off the hills is on a different wavelength from a motorist in a jam. The climber is tired, hungry, but experiencing that wonderful sense of peace that comes only from the hills. The man in the car is not tired, but livery, and is experiencing that terrible sense of negative endeavour caused by the lorryload of sheep that he has been trying to overtake for seventeen miles.

But that day we did not go down on to the road. We headed through the remote Glas loughs and over a small cliff to the old Road again. We climbed south up to the col and wondered whether we should take in the lowly Knockanaguish to its east, for that, clearly, was a hill so unimportant that we would not otherwise climb it. Eventually we decided against peak-bagging and returned to Gowlane. A modest journey of five hours.

That old Kenmare–Killarney Road makes a fine trip in its own right: the more so if you include Torc Mountain in the traverse. Section one, from Gowlane to Galway's river, is quite straightforward and you cross giant stepping stones over the Ullauns river. From a shaking rock, which Barrington calls 'particularly fine' and which I never found, you must try to discern a track going east to Esknamucky Glen. It starts on a rocky shoulder and was marked, in 1979, with red paint. It's easy to miss, and on my first trip I crossed the col north of Stumpacommeen, missing the glen altogether. I was luckier on the second attempt.

The glen is a magical place, with weird boulder formations and dwarf oaks growing out of them. When I left it I failed to find the Corres cascade, though the river was obvious and wet enough. Half a mile after that the road reappears. It is motorable by Land Rover. Torc Mountain towers up ahead of you. The climb is very straightforward: once more there is a route marked, with blue paint. The view from the top over Killarney's lakes is all that the guidebooks make it out to be. Immediately below you are the smooth lawns of the Muckross estate. Tourists in side-cars travel its neat driveways. But it would be a grave mistake to leave Torc direct for Muckross. It is steep woodland choked with vegetation. Our route off was south-east, and I see that I described it as 'a forty five degree gorse boulder field'. It was certainly my nastiest descent from any Kerry hill. Far better, with hindsight, to retrace one's steps to the blue track to the west.

We continued on down the Old Road and soon came to a barrier put up by the Forestry Commission to stop people driving up here. Then we descended to Torc waterfall, thick with trippers and not much of a cascade if you have already seen those that tumble into Coum Fhasaig and the Black Valley. Here, with organisation, you should find your second car. There were eight in our party split into an east team and a west team. Thus half of us did that route in reverse and, I gather, actually found the Corres cascade, though not the shaking rock.

Barrington is keen on these split walks. He recommends that 'you exchange car keys on the ridge'. I've always been a bit nervous of not meeting up with the other group. Lately we've taken to hiding the keys: perhaps in the hub cap, perhaps under the flap by the petrol tank. That's only in the last two years though. Before then we always left cars unlocked with keys in and never had any trouble.

The route is thirteen miles and takes four and a half hours without Torc, six and a half with it.

We are now in Coleman territory. For other Kerry hills the best guide is Sean O'Suilleabhain's. But for Mangerton, J.C. Coleman's *Mountains of Killarney*[2] is essential reading. For he fell in love with this area, and used to bicycle here from Cork. He camped in the centre of volcanic activity, on the shores of Lough Guitane.

Coleman describes the area south of Torc as 'Featureless, with three tops over 2,000 feet. They are in a rise of ground south-west of Mangerton, where that great hill moves down to lower levels. It is a region of no great attraction to the climber. Rather it is a region to walk over.' I had a day around Dromderalough (2,139 ft) and I agree with him. This is simply part of the huge west shoulder of Mangerton. I drove east as far as I could from the Gowlane cross – only a mile or so. Then I hiked up Knockrower (1,814 ft), through the little lakes to Dromderalough, then back over Knockbrack over the 1,367 foot Coombane. There I stupidly got pounded south of the wood, so I had to swing back north.

That incident apart, it was a wild but featureless day with the

Mangerton

summits hard to find. Dromderalough, surely, is the name of the lough to the north of the trig. point, which is not a true summit in any event. The area would appeal to those who prefer moorland to hill. There are plenty of red deer around. My circuit took five hours.

And so I come to Mangerton itself. This mountain was thought to be the highest in Ireland before the survey was done. It is certainly the biggest.

By turning right one mile north of Muckross you come across a sign that states: 'Mangerton, 2¾ miles'. That is only the distance the road runs, however. There's another four and a quarter miles up the hillside. There's a track marked on the map past Torreencormack battlefield. Here, in Hanmer's[1] vivid phrase, 'The Carties played the Divells in Desmond'. He meant that the two factions of MacCarthy Mor and MacCarthy Reagh fought each other in South Kerry, which was then called Desmond. The Geraldine knight John FitzThomas backed the MacCarthy Mor: indeed he saw much personal advantage in so doing and brought over English troops to ensure victory. But in 1261 his troops were routed by Fingen MacCarthy Reagh at the battle of Callan Glen, near Kilgarvan. FitzThomas and his son were slain. So were eight barons and twenty five knights. Fingen than overran and levelled a dozen castles, including Dunloe and Killorglin.

The next year the English and the MacCarthy Mors tried again, here at Torreencormick. The battle was bloody and inconclusive. Gerald de Roche led the English and was killed, but so was Fingen's brother Cormick. The battlefield is called after him. Those two battles were decisive in the history of Kerry. They partioned Kerry between the Anglo-Norman and Gaelic worlds, and were to keep the English out of South Kerry for 400 years, until the Cromwellian Sir William Petty arrived in the mid 1600s.

I know little of the MacCarthy Mors, but we were married by the MacCarthy Reagh, who was Dean and Chaplain of Balliol College. The Revd Francis MacCarthy Willis Bund was the kindliest of men. He died in 1980.

Leaving the battlefield you slog up the shoulder due south. Mangerton is a mountain that is very wet everywhere except on top. There's a shorter route to the Punch Bowl starting from the old Killarney–Kenmare Road just south of Torc. You simply follow the stream up to the lake. There's not much cliff around the Punch Bowl, despite the map marking. But if you swing north from Mangerton's main summit to the neck between The Bowl and Glenacappul you'll see the biggest cliff in Kerry. Below that is Lough Erhogh, also known as O'Donoghue's Ink Well. It is certainly black as ink on most days. Legend has it that O'Donoghue drank with the devil in his Punch Bowl. They fell to blows over the Land Commission. O'Donoghue lost the fight and took flight. The devil plucked a piece of rock from Torc, still marked on the map as Devil's Bit, and threw it at O'Donoghue, but he missed. You will find the rock in Muckross Lake, called Devil's Island.

If you like that sort of story there's another one about Charles

Mangerton, 'Very wet everywhere except on top'

Fox who dived into the Punch Bowl and telexed for his clothes from Australia.

But so far I have done no justice to Mangerton at all. Stories of indecisive battles and dubious legend are no match for the real thing: an ascent up Mangerton through Glenacappul, or the Horse's Glen. To go that way you do not take the road marked 'Mangerton 2¾': you carry on to the Owgarriff bridge and turn right. There's a friendly farmer half a mile on who will mind your car. You travel up a boreen which eventually peters out by the first of the lakes: Garagarry. And then the lowering cliffs of Mangerton close in on either side as you battle your way in through the portals of the glen.

As Coleman[2] before me, I will quote from *Wright's Geological Survey*:

Mangerton. The col between the Punch Bowl and the Horse's Glen

The Devil's punch bowl

83

Most of the mountains in the neighbourhood of Killarney which were not over-ridden by the great ice sheet nourished local glaciers in their higher valleys. One of the most active of these occupied the Horse's Glen between Mangerton and Stoompa. At the margins of this Glen the smooth pre-glacial surface of the mountain breaks away into rugged cliffs over 1,000 feet high: the great cliffs above Lough Erhogh being especially magnificent. The bottom of the glen is occupied by three small lakes about a third of a mile long and three hundred yards wide. The floor is extremely uneven and descends in two well marked steps from its upper corrie at 1,414 feet, to where it opens on the northern slopes of Mangerton at a height of 869 feet. Lough Erhogh occupies the floor of the corrie above the upper rock barrier. There is an accumulation of moraine on the barrier which has undoubtedly raised the level somewhat. The middle lake, Lough Managh, lies above the lower valley step and appears entirely held in by rock barrier. The lower lake, Garagarry, is retained by the great mass of moraine that the glacier laid down at the mouth of the glen. No piece of scenery can show better within so small a compass the extraordinary manner in which a local glacier of no great size can eat into the very heart of a great mountain mass.

There's a track, of sorts, down the east side of Garagarry. The going is rough and wet over fern-smothered boulders. It is an easy thing to do damage by popping a leg down a crevice in the stones. In three-quarters of a mile the valley floor narrows and the flanks of Stoompa and Mangerton North bristle with crags.

At Lough Managh the corrie bends east, and the next mile is the roughest to be met with on Mangerton. There are 'glaciated crags, tumbled boulders, fern and bracken-covered stones and unwelcome wet patches to keep your mind at work.'[2] Only when you reach Erhogh can you pay full attention to the south side of the corrie. Coleman has studied Glenacappul's mighty south side, and describes it as follows:

Eastward are the stony slopes of Stoompa over Managh and there is a stone shoot at the turn of the glen where next are the slabs. A big gully comes down by them, and coming more westward a series of boiler plates, and in places, damp and grassy rock faces. South of the Erhogh stream these die out and then there are stepped slopes leading up to the beginnings of the finest series of cliffs to be met with in Killarney.

Two prominent gullies which I call East and West Gulley scar the cliffs, and around these gullies are magnificent buttresses. Over the south west corner of the lake are the 'lake cliffs': a series of wet connected slabs, with bedding planes sloping around thirty degrees. The west side of the lake runs up in a steep slope scarred with stony gullies, to the col, the other side of which is the Devil's Punch Bowl.

Coleman goes on to describe two grassy tracks that slope upwards through the cliffs to the Punch Bowl col. It is not clear if he has been up this way (I have not). He speaks of many grand opportunities for the rock climber, in particular West Gully: 'Unclimbed so far as I can ascertain'.

Our route lay up the north of the glen, to a peak of *c.* 2,500 feet, which is Coleman's 'Mangerton North'. This is a puff and blow, but there's no cliff, despite the map marking. That day black cloud was massing at 2,300 feet. Our peak was in mist, but the Punch Bowl col just ducked clear of it.

Very suddenly we gained the crest and the mist cleared. We looked beyond Killarney's lakes to the North Kerry plain. Then we struck south to the Punch Bowl col, and I remember how disappointed we were with the Punch Bowl, as we had expected it to be sheerer than the Horse's Glen. Beyond it, Mangerton's main plateau was still fogbound and we set about the most careful compass work, for we knew that the hill was flat and we did not know if there was a cairn. So we did a military march. One man forward on a bearing to the limit of the back man's visibility, then a shout to the front man 'Four paces right' or 'Six paces left' to put him spot on the bearing. After four legs of this we heard the front man shout 'There's a cairn', and we closed in on him. The cairn is only a few piled rocks beside a concrete trig. point. Around it people have spelt their names in patterns of stone. You see 'Peter' and 'James' writ large on the hillside.

And so, sad that we'd 'viewed the mist but missed the view', we returned on a back bearing. We went back over the col to Mangerton North and down its north shoulder to Garagarry and a swim. That trip took five and a quarter hours.

A couple of years later we did much the same trip but went high early on, over Stoompa (2,281 ft). The day was cloudless and the trudge up the twin peaked Stoompa seemed endless. It was one of those hot days when the ants moved *en masse* to the absolute summits of the mountains. They plagued us on Stoompa, so we pushed on south and found the perfect lunch spot by a stream tumbling off the summit plateau into the mighty corrie of Glenacappul.

Two miles away we could see the main summit; only fractionally higher than the plateau. I had read that the view was unbeatable, but when we got there we found two things: first that this hill is so flat that the view is mainly of the rest of it, and second that there was a hornets' nest in the cairn. These pursuing us, we beat a dignified retreat north.

From Mangerton Main to Mangerton North, with the North Kerry Plains beyond

We circuited the Horse's Glen over Mangerton North and dropped down to Garagarry. That trip took six and a quarter hours; longer than the Horse's Glen, and not as impressive really.

I must conclude this description of Mangerton ('the hairy one') with an account of its ascent by Isaac Weld, a verbose Victorian traveller who had already been hauled up a minor Reek by a guide, believing it to be Carrauntoohill:

> I had to cross the plain of Mangerton on the way back to Killarney. On advancing, the air became obscure and at last such dense vapours enveloped us that it was impossible to distinguish an object at the distance of a few yards. Under these circumstances we continued to walk, for more than two hours, over an unvaried surface, where no track whatsoever was visible; our guide still

asserting that he was leading us home by the shortest possible route. The mist soon penetrated our clothes and we began to experience all the inconvenience of wet and cold when the guide, suddenly stopping, took off his coat, turned it inside out, and again deliberately put it on. We marvelled very much at this extraordinary proceeding, and his reluctance to give a satisfactory reply to our inquiries into the motives of it served but to excite still greater curiosity. At last, being pressed for an explanation, he acknowledged that he was totally ignorant of our situation, and had turned his coat as a charm of potent influence to enable a lost man to recover his way. The intelligence was unwelcome. The day was fast approaching to a close, and there was a danger of our taking the very opposite course to that which ought to be followed.[7]

Mr Weld finally descended into Cappagh Glen, all of nine miles from Killarney Town.

Cappagh was a favourite of Coleman's, and the next walk in the Mangerton range takes it in. 'I'm going to Cappagh for a load of hake' is a Killarney man's way of saying 'I'm going to see a man about a dog.'

North of Cappagh is the lovely unspoilt Lough Guitane. 'Seven miles south-east of Killarney is a lake about which very few people know anything', writes Coleman. 'To many it is only a signpost on the Kenmare road and a promise to visit the lough sometime. But for me the lough and its southern garland of hills was my first love and still holds its place. Many times have I camped by the shore after a hurried cycle ride from Cork, preparatory to a few days in the hills, and principally the valleys, which are the attractions of the land south of Guitane'.

So without much doubt Guitane was the area of youthful endeavour and discovery for Coleman. (My own, you must have guessed, was in the valleys of Cummeengeera and Glanrastel on Beara.) Coleman's enthusiastic detail on the routes round here can only emanate from the certain knowledge that he was the young pioneer, doing walks that no man had done before him.

The centrepiece is Bennaunmore, which, like Coleman, I will call simply the Ben. It is like a great worn tooth, but only 1,490 feet high. Dwarfed by Mangerton to its west and Crohane to its east, it is nonetheless a remarkable hill. It probably formed the crater of the Guitane volcano and its rocks are of felstone. This igneous rock forms polygonal columns on the Ben's east side. It is Kerry's Giant's Causeway.

To its west it throws down a considerable cliff into Cappagh, and

Felstone columns on Bennaunmore

here is a petrified forest of dwarf oak. Cappagh is a valley hidden from the north and it is therefore likely that these trees escaped Sir William Petty's hatchet: a hatchet that denuded the rest of Iveragh and Beara for the sake of his iron-smelting furnaces.

If you follow that sign on the Kenmare road marked 'Guitane' you travel the lough's northern shore and you can then branch southward through four gates and leave your car on the shady eastern bank. Here we did the 'Coleman preferred' circuit of the Ben. That is, up Glan Nabroda, over the Ben's south top (not the higher north top, for that is a cul-de-sac) and down steeply into the hidden valley of Cappagh.

Up Nabroda it is rough. Bits of polygonal column have broken off and lie concealed in the high heather. Coleman remarks that this is tough going in summer and recommends the spring, so we took his advice. But that spring day was no better, for it was snowing. High heather laden with snow is chilly material to wade through; the more so when those big bouldery pieces of broken column lie concealed beneath it.

The sight of the Ben's east wall makes it worth while. The columns stretch for a quarter of a mile and are some 200 feet high. Only from a distance do they look regular and slender. Close to, they are of rough stuff and only a few are regular polygons. 'These cliffs', says the expert, 'are not safe for climbing. The columns have a disconcerting habit of coming away piecemeal from the cliff face, and the inviting ledges and jug handle holds are a delusion and a snare.'

When we got to Lough Nabroda we found its outlet stream disappearing beneath our feet. The whole of the valley floor, under the heather, is a great pile of scree, and so the stream runs underground and can be heard but not seen. We walked down the east shore of the lough, where there is a track, used by the pilgrims to Gougane Barra on Gougane Sunday. It is now hard to follow. Further on is a second lough, called variously Crohane or Carrig-begha, and from here you look south to the mountains of Beara rising beyond the neat town of Kilgarvan. Reputedly there is an ice-smooth rock with pilgrims' names and initials carved on it, 'on the western side of Crohane lake, up under a big crag with an inviting chimney in its face'. Coleman 'did not examine these in detail'. Sean O'Suilleabhain could not find them at all, and neither could I.

Now we climbed the few hundred feet to the Ben's south

Cappagh Glen

summit and set about plunging down into Cappagh. Its southern end is cliff bound, with 'a fine tumble of waters on the air'. The valley is choked with fern and moss-covered boulders, and that is dangerous stuff to traverse, unless you feel your way slowly and poke about with sticks. So we went half a mile north to the col between the Ben's two summits and dropped down quite easily until we reached the petrified forest: gaunt leafless trees that snapped off like matchwood in our hands.

Cappagh Glen we found sunny and friendly. The younger trees were just coming into leaf. To our right the wall of the Ben towered smoothly. Up it, says Coleman, is many a fine rock route. The valley floor is green and spacious, but further north it narrows to an 'inch' and is choked with fallen boulders. Beyond that neck it widens again and we simply followed the Cappagh River to Lough Guitane and forded it.

This is no trip for peak-baggers. We'd only been on one summit, and that a mere 1,300 feet. Yet it is a very fine four hour trip which can be done, of course, in all weathers.

To climb the Ben's North top is certainly a scramble and possibly a rock-climb. I have not done it, but it would seem from the map that you could work your way up from its northern spur, and then traverse south to the col and go down either right or left into Cappagh or Nabroda.

Nor have I ascended Crohane from this side. So once more I quote the expert:

> At the south-east corner of Lough Guitane the track way passes under a prominent knoll, deep in fern, and from here it is an hour's good going to make Crohane's little cairn at 2,162 feet. There is very little to be said about the climb: the obvious shoulder running up from the lake shore and turning eastward near the summit is its course.

But once I climbed up Crohane from the south. That was a memorable day, as it was the only fine one we had in a three week holiday. In the morning we'd shot up Knocknagree in the Cahas. In the afternoon some of our party had to catch the Cork boat, so I cadged a lift and was dropped in the Loo valley where the Kenmare and Killarney roads join. That gave me three hours to make the round trip before the car returned. And so I struck over Carrigawaddra.

The lower slopes here are exceedingly rocky and vegetated. Soon I gained a great waste of featureless ground, with many a rocky shoulder between me and Crohane. I must have walked for two miles without gaining much height before I reached the south ridge, and this was a big pull to a rather fine summit pyramid. As I emerged from the cloud-bound Loo Valley it was magnificent to see the whole of Killarney and its Reeks spread out before me. As is often the case, the North Kerry plain was in sun. But I could not linger, for I had cut things fine. I ran back down to the Kenmare road to see, to my great satisfaction, the car approaching as I hit the tarmac.

The valley running north from here is Glen Flesk. The river Flesk is the main feeder of Killarney's lower lake. From its south-east corner rise a jumble of cliffs, and in them is another Robber's Den. In the nineteenth century this den was on the programme of all tourist excursions. The Victorians scaled it with the help of guides, ropes and ladders. But now there are none of these luxuries: instead there is holly, ash, beech, bramble, whitethorn, black-thorn, ferns, heather, grass, and winged nasties in season. So you sweat up through the vegetation and should arrive at a rock shelf with a tree stump at its edge. This is roughly in the middle of the semicircle of cliffs. The den is above this ledge under an over-hanging piece of rock thirty feet above you. The last ten feet to the den is up a smooth face, vertical and almost holdless. There is a horizontal crack half way up which helps – a bit.

Here lived Owen MacCarthy, an ally of that O'Donoghue who argued with the devil in Mangerton's Punch Bowl. Much like the robber of Cummeengeera, Owen was finally caught by a trick. They took him over the Derrynasaggart Mountains and hanged him at Macroom.

The last two peaks of the Mangerton range are more properly in the Derrynasaggarts. They are the Paps of Dana.

Dana was the great mother goddess of the Tuatha De Danaan. The two huge cairns on the Paps' summits must surely have been built as her nipples, for Dana was the goddess of prosperity: a ninth-century tract claims that all of Munster owes its fertility to her. To reach the Paps we left the main road at Clydagh bridge and drove east till we reached the sharp valley dividing them from Knocknabro. This valley is called locally the Sloigeadal. A fair track runs up it, which we followed for three-quarters of a mile, and then we struck up left, through the deepest heather that I have ever travelled. That slog takes no more than half an hour.

We reached the first 'nipple'. It is around fifteen feet high and has a modern cairn on top of it. Thence we plunged down to the col and looked down to an icy lake: Athooynastooka. From here a surprising knife edge only three feet high took us up the western Pap. The 'nipple' on top of that one is somewhat smaller and at its base is a sheep-shelter where we had lunch. Then the cloud came down and we escaped by compass over Rodger's Rock. This is, simply, a good view-point for watching sheep on the hillside, and the boy whose job it was to do that when the British Engineers were drawing their maps was called Rodger.

The Paps only take three hours to traverse. East of them the mountains end. True, there are high points like Caherbanagh and Musheramore, but they are no more than rolling upland. The point of the Paps traverse is, without doubt, the view, particularly from the western Pap. I quote Coleman:

> Nowhere in Kerry can you see to such perfection the two major divisions of the kingdom: the massing of its southern highlands and the northern lowlands and plain stretching to the Shannon. Vividly you can see the meeting place of Hill and Plain, that long escarpment of the geological overfold stretching past Killarney.
> The hills we have climbed are now ranged solidly before our view and a more fitting place to take farewell of them could hardly be found.
> But if I had the choice of introducing a new recruit to the hills, I would bring him up on the Paps and let him see the mountains of Killarney and let the glory of the scene speak louder than any words of mine.

That concludes the walks in the Mangerton range. The glory of Killarney's highest mountains lies ahead.

4. MacGillycuddy's Reeks

The MacGillycuddies are a sept of the O'Sullivan Mors. Until recently they lived at the foot of the mountains over which their ancestors hunted deer and wild boar. The Reeks are not the only Irish Mountains so named, for in Mayo there is Croagh Patrick which is known simply as 'The Reek'. It is probably a corruption of 'Rick'.

The Ricks, or Reeks, cover some thirty square miles, and are set apart from Iveragh's main backbone by the Bridia col which joins the Caragh valley to the Black Valley. There is a western horseshoe and an eastern ridge. The horseshoe contains the three highest peaks in Ireland, and the ridge the fourth highest. Around the shoe rise Carrauntoohill, Beenkeragh, and Caher. The ridge reaches its highest point at Knocknapeasta (3,191 ft) though this is given neither name nor height on the maps.

If you go back to the Ballaghbeama gap, which seems to be the best reference point for all Iveragh, you will see the Reeks towering up to your right a few miles north of it. Take the road right up the Caragh (Bridia) valley. A fairly simple circuit of Caher and Carrauntoohill starts here.

To begin with there's an almighty slog up the south face of Curraghmore. Towards the top it's a bit cliffy but there are gullies

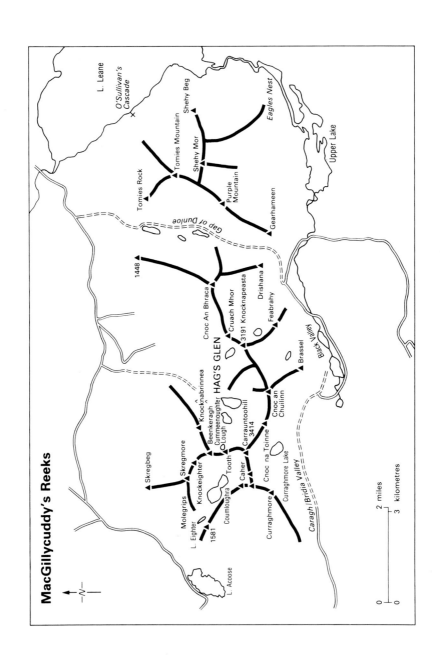

MacGillycuddy's Reeks

L. Leane
O'Sullivan's Cascade
Tomies Mountain
Shehy Beg
Shehy Mor
Tomies Rock
Eagles Nest
Tomies Mountain
Shehy Mor
Purple Mountain
Upper Lake
Gearhameen
Gap of Dunloe
1448
Cnoc An Bhraca
Cruach Mhor
Drishana
3191 Knocknapeasta
Feabrahy
Knocknabrinnea
HAG'S GLEN
Beenkeragh
Cummeenoughter
Lough
Brassel
Black Valley
Skregbeg
Skregmore
Carrauntoohill
3414
Cnoc an Chuilinn
Molegrips
Knockeighter
Tooth
Caher
Cnoc na Toinne
L. Eighter
1581
Coumloughra
Curraghmore
Curraghmore Lake
Caragh |Bridia Valley
L. Acoose

0   2 miles
0   3 kilometres

Carrauntoohill

through the rock. I reckon it takes one and a half hours to gain Curraghmore's rather flat top. At 2,695 feet it is the highest hill I have so far described, but there's higher stuff beyond it. Coleman calls it the Cinderella of the Reeks. Well, it's a boring shoulder and deserves that name. Perhaps I dislike it because we have aborted so many Carrauntoohill ascents from its shoulder. The slog is behind us: ahead lies ridge-walking unequalled in Ireland. But low cloud and horizontal hail force us to crawl back down the gully.

A fine day in Kerry does not mean a fine day on the Reeks. Often have we set out with high hopes and a cloudless sky, and only as we breasted the top of the Carriganine Pass have we seen a great splurge of grey over the Reeks. We tend to press on, as we're psyched up for the trip, and it's still an hour and a half's drive away. 'Clearing fast' we say. But when we get to Bridia and the weather gets worse we sometimes press up Curraghmore hoping

Curraghmore shoulder with Caher beyond

for the best, or sometimes strike right up Broaghnabinnea as a soft option. That peak is nearly always clear of cloud. However, if in luck on the Curraghmore shoulder, the walk on to Caher East (it has two summits) is over easy grass. From Caher there is a path which drops steeply to the lip of Coumloughra. You now traverse a very narrow ridge. Weird black gullies drop out of sight to the north. Sometimes there is cloud in the coum below, and the view is of a wicked abyss vanishing in a hell's cauldron of vapour.

It's an easy amble now up to the 'roof of all Ireland': the 3,414 foot summit of Carrauntoohill. Even if you're up here on a sunny August afternoon you will probably have it to yourselves. A description of the view would be a comprehensive listing of every Kerry peak, so I will mention only the extremities: the Paps, Hungry Hill, Mullaghanattin and Brandon. Northward you can see beyond the Kerry plain over the Shannon to Clare and even into Galway.

Carrauntoohill's top has a massive cairn and a steel cross. Erected in 1977 by the people of Tuogh, the cross was intended as a permanent symbol of their faith. It replaced the original timber cross put up in the Holy Year of 1950.[7] I remember stories of the ladies of Killarney following the priest up to bless that cross in their Sunday best and high-heeled shoes. There was many a sprained ankle, and worse. So many of those who climb Carrauntoohill seem to have no concept that it is a serious mountain. I said that you would meet no one on the summit: if I'm wrong, the person you do meet will have neither map nor compass and will be wearing wellingtons. It is hardly surprising that there are more accidents on Carrauntoohill than on the rest of Kerry's peaks put together. And such people, I regret, are bad on litter. The summit is a dirty place of Coke tins and orange peel. Please do a service to your fellow travellers and at least remove some of it.

The route off Carrauntoohill is down a badly cairned track to the top of the Devil's ladder. On the map a road is marked to its top, but that is more cartographic fiction. We go down the back of the ladder very steeply to Curraghmore Lough. It's worth looking up to the southern flank of the Caher ridge. It is a nasty vegetable cliff. Thus there is no way off the ridge save over the summits of Carrauntoohill or Caher.

In Curraghmore lake I once had the best swim of my life. The lake is only a thousand feet high and is warmed by the sun. We'd breasted Carrauntoohill on a September day blistering hot with not a puff of wind, even on the summit, and we had no water. One man had an orange, and the going rate for that was fifty pence a piece.

What could be closer to heaven than to peel off one's gear, soaked in sweat, and then to feel all the filth and grot washed off you by the blue waters of Curraghmore? And as you swim you drink. That day we swam nude. We did not know of the ancient Irish taboo on nudity, which stems from 1700 BC and Milesius's grandson Luigdeach's nude swim in Lough Currane. His wife, Fial, was also swimming naked in the little river that runs from the lake. Husband and wife confronted each other unexpectedly, and Fial died of shame. So it is perhaps prudent to chuck a pair of bathing trunks into your rucksack.

Curraghmore Lake, with the Reeks on the left

And so refreshed, relaxed, we sauntered down from the Bridia col and were back at our car in five and a half hours. Incidentally, every route up Carrauntoohill seems to take that sort of time.

If you follow the main Ballaghbeama road north you come to the Waterville–Killarney road, and three miles on you see the whole cirque of Ireland's highest peaks reflected in the waters of Lough Acoose, which is itself 500 feet above sea level. Immediately north of the lake a tarred road winds over the hillside. This is the old Lack Road, connecting Acoose with the Bridia valley. It forms a section of the new 'Kerry Way': a footpath that will eventually circuit the whole of Iveragh.

A mile and a half further north is another road that services the Cottoners River Hydro Electric Scheme. That road makes a good approach to the Reeks. It takes you up to Lough Eighter in Coumloughra. From this lake descend two pipes: a six inch main, which is the water supply for Killorglin, and an eighteen inch main to power the generators by Cottoner's River. The electricity so made is fed into the National Grid. But this road has an unfriendly gate across it and a sign reading 'Private Road: Works in progress'. It may be better to start from a farmhouse and clump of firs just beyond it.

Wherever you start, you are about to embark on Kerry's finest walk, the *Coomloughra Horseshoe*. We did it one typical summer's day: clear everywhere, cloud on the Reeks. It started with a boring half hour slog up uneven heather. We saw above us a rock to the west of Skregmore which we christened Molegrips from its shape. Another forty five minutes found us puffed on top of it. The cloud hid the ridge ahead, but we pressed on. The ridge is narrow and quite difficult to miss. One of the advantages of mist is that you can only see the next fifty feet of ascent, so you never have the feeling that the top is miles away. And so suddenly we found ourselves on Skregmore's summit, and, a little later, on Knockeighter's.

All the time it was getting darker. I began to get the matador feeling about finding the knife edge that connects Beenkeragh to Carrauntoohill. The phrase 'matador feeling', I should explain, comes from my brother Andrew, who was round the back of a Spanish bullring one day and saw six young matadors fully togged up sitting in a Cadillac waiting for their fights. They did not talk at all: they wore masks of keen apprehension. Blind panic would perhaps be too strong a phrase, for matadors are fearless. Anyhow, I had that feeling, and my brother David said calmly, 'Soon it will rain rather hard'.

He was right. Five minutes later the hillside was awash with the fiercest storm I have known. It was a flash storm of the kind that can raise river levels by ten feet in as many minutes. If you look at the river gorges cutting out of Coomloughra, or the Hag's Glen, you will see the banks scoured clean and vertical for twenty feet by the flash floods of the Reeks.

Up on the ridge stair-rods of water cut through our anoraks instantly. We could have been standing under Torc Cascade in spate. Visibility was down to a couple of feet as the rain turned to a stinging hail. In seconds the hillside was white and there was a mighty flash and clap of thunder and lightning. 'Down!' I yelled. But which way? We got out the map, which was waterlogged before we'd opened it. It was hard to read the compass through my streaming glasses, so we slithered down a slope covered with vast hailstones, not really certain of where we'd find ourselves when we'd cleared cloud.

In ten minutes we looked down on a valley with two lakes in it and we had here a difference of opinion, for some said it was Coumloughra (good news), and I thought it was the Hag's Glen (less good news). And so I tried to get people to climb back over the ridge into the right valley, but there were no takers. The hail now eased and we looked at the map less hurriedly. True, Coumloughra on the map had only one big lake, but that was an hourglass shape. We were looking at two lakes of the right shape but separated by a bank of scree. When I looked at the Hag's Glen lakes on the map I saw that they were widely separated. We had to be in Coumloughra.

The cloud suddenly cleared Caher opposite, and we saw an extraordinary sight. Four ribbons of foaming white poured down its mighty cliff, but half way down they stopped. The storm had been so violent but so short that the waters had just not had time, yet, to reach the bottom of the cliff. And so we went down to the lake shore. It was a steep descent, but, being in Iveragh, it was grass.

We stopped by the lake and looked at Caher's streaming north wall, and we wondered whether there could be rock-climbing there. I have subsequently discovered that the answer is yes.

> Climbs varying from 500 to 1,000 feet are to be had, though generally it is impossible to make direct ascents; but traverses are practicable so eventually the Caher ridge above is attained.

So writes Coleman.[2] It is not absolutely certain that he has climbed Caher's north wall except in his mind. But undoubtedly H.C. Hart[4] did so at the end of the last century:

> The rock is sound and a fine, an almost vertical ascent of 1,000 feet may be made striking the ridge of Caher 200 feet below the summit. It is a severe climb and very long, entailing many zigzags. There is no main gully to adhere to and the cliffs are less impracticable than they look.

We walked out of Coumloughra, passing the narrow Lough Eighter. Below it a flash flood has caused a landslip. Soon we gained a good wide track, but it petered out as these tracks often do. I was wearing jeans and was thoroughly cold. Indeed jeans are the very worst things to wear on the hills, for once they are wet they lose all their warmth and are like so many wet fish brushing your legs. And they don't dry out, either. We were on the hill for five and three quarter hours that day.

Three days later we were slogging up Skregmore to 'Molegrips' again. And the weather was clear everywhere. When we'd gained Skregmore's summit we saw ahead of us three peaks. The next one we knew was called Knockeighter, the one beyond had evidently no name, and the furthest was Beenkeragh.

From Skregmore onwards the going is really most pleasant. It is over a large flat sort of scree. To the north is a tempting glen with sides of sheer black rock, but according to Hart,[4] 'These cliffs are to be avoided. At several points an attempt was made to scale them, but the rock is most rotten.'

The ascent of Beenkeragh is up awkward boulders and takes a while. We looked down on Coumloughra and I felt pretty foolish about mistaking it for the Hag's Glen. The prospect south of Beenkeragh is daunting. The mountain falls away steeply to a col and arising from that is the knife edge of nunataks that Coleman calls 'The finest ridgewalk in all Ireland'.

We traversed a three-pronged minor summit that Sean O'Suilleabhain calls the Tooth. The ridge is choppy indeed, and we needed our hands and a head for heights. For the more cautious there is a route of sorts below the ridge on the Coumloughra side for the first two thirds of it. My brother Andrew got stuck on at least one of the vertical pitches and developed a condition that he called 'quiver thigh'. In truth, this ridge is easier than the Aonach Eagach in Glencoe and does not have the exposure of the Crib Goch in Snowdonia.

As we neared Carrauntoohill we saw down to our left the Devil's Looking Glass Lake in the hanging valley of Cummeenoughter. It would be easy enough to get down to it from Beenkeragh: there's even a wall above it to keep the sheep away from the cliff. Indeed one of these days I'd like to climb Carrauntuohill by Cummeenoughter. The route up to it from the Hag's Glen is up huge dangerously sloping slabs.

The lake (says Hart) is at 2,500 feet and is three parts encircled by a fine series of cliffs. Excellent climbing is to be had here. The rock is of purple sandstone, and one shoulder of inaccessible appearance can be climbed throughout, owing to the firmness of grip and suggestive little footholds. The Hag's Teeth, in contrast, are conical knobs of no difficulty.

The Beenkeragh/Carrauntoohill section of the Coumloughra circuit.
Note: (a) Cross on Carrauntoohill's summit. (b) Party on the ridge and
(c) Hungry Hill in the distance

The main nunatak ridge merges into the north face of Carraun-toohill. A track leads steeply up, but this is disintegrating and is better avoided.

The summit itself I have already described, and from the littered top of the 'roof of all Ireland' we simply walked steeply down the tourist track for a while until it became quite obvious that we must strike right to gain the Caher ridge. It is tame compared to the nunataks, but still a deal more airy than anything away from the Reeks.

We traversed on to Caher West, or Caher Pinnacle. Due west of that, easy slopes go down to Acoose. We met here a Dutch family. They had a road map, wore gym shoes, and their child was

A hag's tooth. A 'Conical knob of no difficulty' (Hart)

My brother Andrew with 'Quiver Thigh'

103

carrying a yellow plastic bag that evidently contained duty-free.

'Which is the way to the top?' they asked.

'Of what?' I asked in return.

'Hgochuntewl,' was the approximate reply and I said, 'Too far. Too dangerous. Go just to Caher.'

I hope that that is all they did.

As we left the Dutch we swung down towards trig. point 1,581, and the circuit grew quite tame. Indeed there seemed little point in continuing over the trig. point so we dropped down north to the lough. Ankle-breaking scree slowly gave way to grass. We crossed the stream flowing into Lough Eighter and descended through gorse and heather past many a fine waterfall.

The circuit of Coumloughra is a fine trip indeed. It took us six and a half hours that day, though I have it on record that I managed four hours and twenty minutes when I had just returned from the Alps in 1952.

That day we were to meet up with friends for drinks by Caragh Lake. As we pitched on to their lawn in our sweaty shorts and muddy boots we found a group eating and drinking who clearly had no need to do either. They sipped at cocktails and nibbled at biscuits. Our approach was less refined. When offered biscuits we took handfuls. When offered choice of drink I said 'apple juice' and downed the miniature glass offered without so much as a swallow. How finely tuned are the bodies of those on a light programme. When they say that they feel like a drink they have no climber's thirst for it, and when they claim to feel cold they have not lost all feeling in their feet. I behave in the same way when I'm not climbing. Discomfort is a subjective condition dependent entirely on what one is achieving. As for drink on the hills, I'm reminded of a local enthusiast's description of the water in the Devil's Punch Bowl: 'The grandest water in Ireland: just a drop of John Jameson in it and it will go down your throat like a torchlight procession and warm the nails in your boots!'

The next route up Carrauntoohill is the standard or 'tourist' route. It is extremely hard to find, and I can do no better than quote Sean O'Suilleabhain[8] on the approaches:

Two access roads lead south from the road which runs along the north side of the Reeks from Dunloe to Glancuttane. The more westerly one runs over a narrow bridge and left at the Y-junction to lead directly to the green road that takes you deep into the Hag's Glan. The easterly one passes the Carrauntoohill

Youth Hostel (shown on some maps as Gortboy School) and ends in a farmyard at Mealis where, with permission, you could leave your car. From here, with the peak already in view, the line of a pipe can be clearly traced to cross the Gaddagh river and meet the green road.

Which ever route you choose you can now continue along the road besides which runs the pipe line (it also marks a new better ford) to Lough Callee (Lough Chaillighe: The lake of the Hag). Here can be seen the recently constructed inlet for the Mid-Kerry water supply which is the reason for the fresh scars along the Glen.

As you walk up the glen you have the wild main ridge of the Reeks to your left, and Knocknabrinnea closing in on your right. It becomes steeper and throws out two rocky pinnacles called the Hag's Teeth. Six families used to live up here. Sometimes their homes were swept away by flash floods; the last really big one was

The Hag's Glen, with one of the Hag's teeth on the right. The Devil's ladder climbs to the low col in the middle

The top of the devil's ladder and Cnoc an Chuillin (3,141)

in 1916. One of these people was a 'hag' or possibly an 'unkempt woman' who chased her lover and fell into the Hag's Lake, presumably parting with her teeth (false?) on Knocknabrinnea.

This indeed is the tourist route up Ireland's highest mountain. But do not be surprised if you have the valley to yourself. Would that one could have the same in England or Scotland! Ahead of you is the great grassy cliff of Carrauntoohill's north-east face. The col to its left contains the grey streak of the Devil's Ladder. It's an hour from the car to its base.

The Victorian guides described the ladder as 'as near vertical as makes no difference'. In truth it's an easy gully with tiresome sliding scree, and you're up it in twenty minutes. From the top of the ladder there is still another 1,250 feet of ascent. The route is dotted with cairns. It's a boring slog, much like the west side of Mullaghanattin, but it is safe.

Should the mist come down when you have gained the top the only sensible way off this hill is back down the cairned route, but when we last climbed up this way it was clear and we decided to traverse back over Beenkeragh and Knocknabrinnea. The latter is an unloved Reek rarely traversed. The advantage of our route was that we were staying high on a very hot day; and we took in the nunatak ridge.

We could not stop long on Carrauntoohill for there was a plague of flying ants in the summit cairn. The ridge traverse was as delightful as ever (we did it topless) and on top of Beenkeragh we found a similar plague of nasties. The way off it down to Knocknabrinnea is over a steep boulder field. Our water supply was by now exhausted and we tried to squeeze some muddy liquid from sphagnum bog on the col. It tasted fruity.

Knocknabrinnea has three summits. Each one was infested with flying ants: perhaps they too were suffering from the heat and had come up in search of a breeze. There was none. We dropped off Knocknabrinnea which is really rather a non-event of a mountain and made it back to the car in six hours.

You go exactly the same way up the Hag's Glen if you wish to traverse the Ridge of the Reeks: a walk which is in some ways finer than Coumloughra, as there's a sting in the tail. You turn left at the top of the ladder, and it's a bit of a sweat up Cnoc na Toinne (2,776 ft). As you traverse its flat top you see a bigger sweat ahead, up the steep grass of Cnoc an Chuillin (3,141 ft). There is a fence and gate across the hillside here. Once over the 3,000 foot contour the going is flat and the grass as good as Wimbledon's. We considered once what a good place this would be for tennis courts, though a ball hit out of court north would fall a good 1,200 feet into Lough Cummeenmore.

You traverse two other summits now; the last of these is the highest of the ridge: Knocknapeasta, 3,191 feet, but not marked at all on the map. Ahead of you lies the 'sting in the tail': another rocky nunatak ridge like the one connecting Beenkeragh to Carrauntoohill. Again the knife edge can be avoided, mainly to the south, but the true Gael will keep the top of the ridge aligned with the seam of his trousers and this gives an airy scramble indeed. The ridge is called An Grean.

The first time I was along here I had a stick, and this proved an

Gap of Dunloe with Purple Mountain (left)
and the Ridge of the Reeks (right)

infernal nuisance. I put it in my rucksack; it fell out. I stuck it in my belt, but it kept fouling the rocks. Yet sticks on these hills are by and large useful, both as a third leg and for probing bog. Only recently have I found the answer, and this is the *collapsible* stick that you can buy at Swane and Adeney's, in Piccadilly.

The knife edge climbs to a nameless peak and then swings north. From here on it is, if anything, even sharper. There's a 'funk route' on the left.

The final rocky top is Cruach Mhôr (3,062 ft). On it is a grotto built by an old man from Ballyledder. He hauled everything up here himself in plastic sacks. The water for the cement he brought up in buckets from Lough Cummeenapeasta. Presumably there was once a holy statue here, for this was the Old Man of Ballyledder's shrine. By keeping the cliff on your left you can now swing down to the Lough. We swam in that one too: but beware – it is 2,000 feet up and it gets no sun. We warmed up as we ran down to the car. The walk took six hours.

The Ridge of the Reeks walk as described in most guidebooks starts in the Gap of Dunloe and takes in the lower Knocknabracka (2,398 ft). Furthermore the Kerry Fell Runners do the whole ridge of the Reeks and then the Coumloughra Horseshoe on the first Sunday in July. They finish at Lough Acoose where they get soup and certificates.

The reason I have not steered you this way is because I detest the Gap of Dunloe and all it contains. It is part of the truly awful tourism of Killarney. Everything must be paid for. 'Walk up the road from Kate Kearney's Cottage' say the guidebooks. You'll be lucky. You will more likely have to hire a nag, or even a cart, and during the trip you'll be regaled with what I call 'bogus blarney', like 'Carrauntoohill is 3,413 feet high. We had to saw off the top foot so that the moon could clear it'. The nags are trained to stop at every cafe, at the place where the man blows his trumpet to cause an echo, and of course by the gypsies selling ordinary heather. Thomas Cook reckoned he could beat the system in the nineteenth century and advertised coach trips through the gap. But the way was blocked by boulders. When his drivers cleared these and pressed on, bursts of rifle fire from the cliffs spattered the coaches.

I have driven through the Gap in mid winter. Then it's a wild and awful place, and there are a couple of hummocks in the road which may catch your sump. There are great cliffs on either side and three lakes: but in none of them was the last snake killed by St Patrick. That happened on Skellig.

What I do recommend is a traverse of the Reeks from the Black Valley. We drove just half a mile beyond the Dunloe Gap turn, and here there is not a tout or tripper to be seen. Then we had a good scramble up the little peak of Feabrahy, 1,894 feet and no more than a shoulder. It was a wild day for August, and we had two heavy hail spills. Fortunately there's many a cave in the Feabrahy ridge so we sheltered and stayed dry. We fetched up on the top of Knocknapeasta and then walked along the grassy section. At Cnoc an Chuillin we swung south down a steep grass slope to the flat topped Brassel Mountain (1,888 ft). We looked west to what must surely be the nastiest ascent in Kerry: a 3,000 foot slog up grass from Dromluska to the top of Cnoc an Chuillin. The descent from Brassel is over interesting rock with a fine cliff to the East. That little circuit took us a leisurely four and a half hours.

East of the Gap of Dunloe rises the Purple Mountain group.

Though the highest point is 2,739 feet these are rounded hills of heather and scree, and an anticlimax after the Western Reeks. But being lower and to the east of the main peaks they are often out of cloud when all else is smothered.

Coleman recommends a route out of the Gap of Dunloe from the North. You leave the road where it crosses the river Loe. 'Beware' he warns 'Kate Kearney's Cottage and the dreaded ponies are only a quarter of a mile ahead of you.' The ascent goes over Tomies Rock, where there is about 400 feet of purple sandstone, mostly horizontal in bedding. The whole face inclines slightly backwards. There are fairly regular cross-joints and very little vegetation. It has three well marked buttresses and some detached splinters with loose pieces near their tops: 'the grandest place for rock climbing in the gap' he says.

Thence the route lies over Tomies Mountain, 'Tomies South', with a diversion to Shehy Mor (2,503 ft) and up over Purple Mountain, then down easily at first to the Glas Lough and south-west from there over awkward boiler plates with many a detour to the head of the Gap.

One blustery day in February I walked these tops, but since I had Dunloe Phobia I approached from Tomies Cottage. For that I turned left off the Gap road at Dunloe Lower. I was soon driving up a rough forest track with many a gate, so I took to my feet. Tomies Wood has fine young oak and birch in it. Angling up through the skeletal trees, I thought what a magnificent sight they must make in April as they burst into leaf, with Lough Leane lying placid below them. Even in February the birds were singing, including, I claim, a cuckoo.

Above the wood is the Bourne Vincent Memorial Park, in which are red deer, and to protect the trees from the deer, a ten foot high deer fence which has to be scaled. In 1978 I found it old and full of gaps. I scrambled through up the hillside, and in an hour and a half I was on top of Tomies (North, 2,413 ft). There is a small cairn surrounded by prehistoric graves which give the mountain its name.

The obvious peak due south of me was Coleman's 'Tomies South' (no name or height on map) and away to its east the trig. point 2,503, which Coleman calls Shehy Mor. That peak slopes down to Shehy proper – or Shehy Beg – an 1,800 foot peak directly above the Lower Lake. But that day I gave the Shehys a miss and went on to Purple Mountain. It's crest is narrow and has three cairns: two tumbled affairs at each end and a better one in the middle. The going is over large flat scree similar to the stuff on the Carrauntoohill circuit. It is blue-black in colour, yet looks purple when viewed from afar.

As I headed west it looked so simple just to traverse on to the icy peaks of Cruach Mor and Knocknapeasta. Not till I reached Purple's west end did I see the gulch that prevented me. Its floor was 1,400 feet beneath me. I looked over to the smooth black precipice of Bull Rock and thought of the might of the glacier that had carved out the Dunloe Gap. It was a lateral overflow of the main Killarney glacier. The ice scoured and plucked the rock up to the 1,750 foot contour. It smoothed and scratched it. It set down erratic boulders, often of a different type from the base rock. Thus the Gap was created: a more dramatic example of the power of ice than even Mangerton's Horse's Glen.

I retraced my steps in search of another tourist attraction which looks most dramatic on Victorian prints: O'Sullivan's Cascade. It is formed by the stream that starts below the col between Tomies South and North, and that gave quite an easy descent until I got to the wood. Then it was awkward work following the stream down over mossy boulder and greasy cliff. I crossed the two forest roads. I gained the edge of the lake. No cascade. The stream did tumble steeply through the wood with many a rapid, so I presumed that 'O'Sullivan's Cascade' referred to the whole length of it. But that made the Victorian engravings pure fiction. Then I saw to my north a little quay, and I waded the stream to it. Looking back now, I saw a thin trickle tumbling through tree and cliff to the lake. That was it: the great Victorian attraction, now unloved and unvisited, but with reason, for it is even less of an event than Torc Waterfall. It is, I suppose, possible that it might look like the engravings after four inches of rain; but after storms like that you have a hundred waterfalls to choose from. And so I say reluctantly that O'Sullivan's Cascade is not worth the trip.

The view here is of Innisfallen Island and Killarney town beyond. A rainbow forms over the Pugin cathedral. I fell to reflecting on this place which Barrington describes as having 'all the disadvantages of the Irish town with none of its redeeming features'. It was Lord Kenmare who developed it as a tourist centre: and Queen Victoria's visit in 1861 further boosted its reputation.

Killarney is all wrong [writes Lloyd Praeger[8]] but indeed the wrongnesses are mostly its misfortune, not its fault. In the first place, it stands on the wrong place: on flat ground, with a lake two miles wide and five miles in length cutting you off from the paradise on its southern side: for to west, north and east the district around Killarney is quite dull. Nor does the town stand by the lake shore, but over a mile inland, with the high walls and dense trees of Kenmare demesne preventing for several miles even a glimpse of lake or mountain. The road that leads down to Lough Leane offers the visitor a mile and a half of flat straight dull thoroughfare, with flat fields on one side and a high wall on the other. The other roads leading fom Killarney are dull too. The Kenmare road is somewhat better from the start, but you go four miles before the lovely wooded hills begin'.

Lloyd Praeger continues in this vein, to make the good point that Kenmare is closer to the finest scenery: the Upper Lake, the Long Range, and the Reeks above them. 'Quiet Kenmare, far from the madding crowd' is no longer that, for when Lloyd Praeger described it, it had only the Lansdowne Arms and the Great Southern Hotel. Now it has six modern hotels, and Remy's Restaurant, which is so good that people travel from Cork especially to eat there.

But you can still park your car in Main Street. In Killarney you can park nowhere.

5. The Glenbeigh Horseshoe

The remaining Iveragh hills are indeed far from the madding crowd. If you wend your way from Killarney towards Waterville you pass four miles north of that great reference point, the Ballaghbeama, and you soon gain a pass just as wild: the Ballaghisheen. This is the gap between Knocknagapple and Knocknacusha. To the north curves the famous but neglected Glenbeigh Horseshoe. To the south is the Cloon Circuit which I described under the Dunkerrons.

Ballagh means 'pass' and 'Isheen' is a corruption of 'Oisin', the son of Fionn Mac Cumhail. Oisin learnt to talk with the wild beasts. There is a lovely film bearing his name made by Paddy Carey which you can hire from Contemporary Films.* (Paddy made a grand film on Beara, too, and that one you can also hire or

* 55 Greek Street, London WIV 6DB. Telephone 01-734-4901.

The Northern wing of Glenbeigh horseshoe from across Dingle Bay

perhaps borrow from me!) The Oisin legend is more romantic than most. If you stop at the top of his pass you get a magnificent view east to the Reeks and Mullaghanattin looks quite perpendicular. Here Oisin hunted with his clansmen, the Fianna. One day a beautiful golden-haired girl called Niamh came towards them on a white horse and persuaded Oisin to come with her to her kingdom. They both mounted the horse and galloped towards the sea at Glenbeigh. At the end of Rossbeigh Strand they took to the sea and reached Tir na nOg, the land of eternal youth. They had to cross the narrow neck of water between Rossbeigh and Inch, where roared Tonn Toime, the magical mystery wave that had earlier wrecked the hopes of 'twenty kings looking for kingdoms' sailing in from the Blaskets.

So Oisin stayed with his bride Niamh on Tir na nOg (presumably

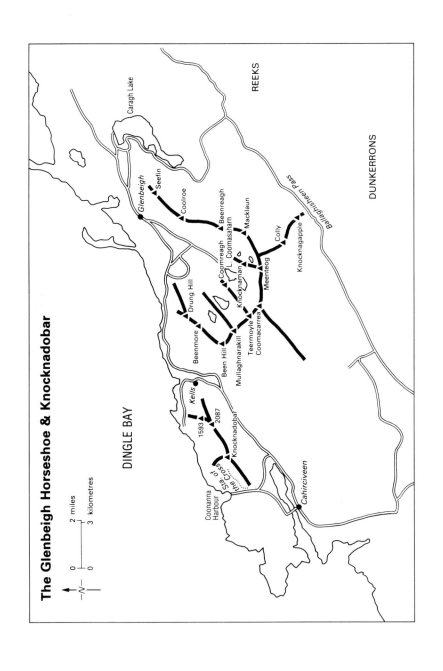

The Glenbeigh Horseshoe & Knocknadobar

DINGLE BAY

REEKS

DUNKERRONS

Caragh Lake

Glenbeigh

Seefin

Coolroe

Beenreagh

Coomreagh

Macklaun

L. Coomasaharn

Knocknaman

Colly

Meenteog

Knocknagapple

Ballaghbeama Pass

Drung Hill

Beenmore

Been Hill

Teermoyle

Mullaghnarakill

Coomacarrea

Kells

1593

2087

Knocknadobar

St's of the Cross

Coonanna Harbour

Cahirciveen

N

0 — 2 miles
0 — 3 kilometres

Dingle) and after a little while decided that he must revisit his people the Fianna. He crossed back through the legendary wave and climbed the Ballaghisheen. He could see no Fianna anywhere, and nor was this surprising, for what seemed to Oisin 'a little while' was in reality 300 years. Niamh had warned him that he would lose his youth if he put foot to land. So he roamed the length and breadth of Ireland on horseback looking for his people. When he was near Dublin he saw a band of puny men trying to shift a boulder. He leaned over and easily lifted the stone, but it broke the horses's girth whereupon Oisin fell to the ground and immediately became a very old man.

The leader of those 'puny men' was St Patrick. And there followed long dialogues between the old pagan, Oisin, and the new Christian Patrick. This is how the great deeds of the Fianna have come to be preserved in writing. The dialogues mirrored the long love-hatred that was to persist between old Gaelic and new Christian cultures. But finally those two great men were reconciled, and St Patrick saved Oisin's soul.

From Ballaghisheen there's a grand trek north on to the horseshoe over Colly to Meenteog and back. With good organisation indeed you could press on and do the whole circuit, ending up at a second car left on the main road north of Drung Hill. I have never been so organised, and estimate that that trip would take a good nine hours. Indeed this shoe is more awkward than it looks, for should you do the obvious thing and leave a car in the Glenbeigh valley both Knocknagapple and Colly are off the circuit, and Colly is the finest of the Glenbeigh peaks. The lowly Knocknagapple is most rocky and takes a surprising one and half hours to traverse. That apart the trip is straightforward enough and the 'out and back' takes five hours.

The head of Glenbeigh Valley is cliff encircled. The cliffs are not as steep as those in the Horse's Glen, and they have a crumbly rotten look about them. It would be easy enough to leave your car at the foot of Lough Coomasaharn and circuit clockwise from Macklaun to Drung Hill. That should take seven and a half hours, plus a rather wet couple of miles across the valley floor. I have not done that either, purely because I happened to be on Meenteog only two days before I was in the valley and did not fancy traversing the same ground twice. So I struck up Coomreagh (locally Conaire, 1,682 ft), a flat lump which narrows dramatically

The head of Glenbeigh Valley

at its junction with Teermoyle. I was between Loughs Coumagla-slaw and the bigger Coomasaharn.

Coomasaharn Lake is of interest. First, there are the famous Coomasaharn scribed stones, five in number, which you reach by turning west by a clump of pines at its foot. These stones bear neolithic writing: concentric circles and, in one place, a cup and single circle linked to a tree system. Second, there is in the lake a peculiar fish, called the Coomasaharn char. Barrington says it resembles a small salmon that never goes to sea. He describes the fishing as 'extensive but temperamental' which suggests that perhaps he has never landed a char. Nor have I.

The rib of rock that joins Coumreagh or Conaire to Teermoyle is strictly a one man pass. It is most precipitous – the rocks look as though they will give way on all sides – and the experience is only made slightly less daunting by a path that traces the safest course.

But once on Teermoyle there is bogland sloping gently westward. This shoe provides the most clear-cut example of the contrast between the peneplain and the ice age coum. From the west the slopes are so gentle that you cannot see the summits, and this is perhaps why the English engineers have here given trig. points that are not summits, merely shoulders. Teermoyle, for instance, is clearly higher than the 2,442 point marked to its left. And in the case of Been Hill the trig. point is one mile west of the true summit and 100 feet below it.

Yet who could believe these hills gentle, regarding them from the east? From that point they number amongst the fiercest in Kerry. The Glenbeigh shoe is somewhat like Mangerton: one huge sloping massif with sharp coums cut out of its very centre by glaciers. The difference between it and 'The Hairy One' is that its lakes are abreast of each other, giving four small coums, whereas Mangerton's are in proper 'line ahead' or paternoster order. Thus Glenbeigh must have had four small glaciers; Mangerton one large one. It would be bad news to lose the way on Glenbeigh in mist. All descents to the valley east are precipitous and rotten. One would have to go west: safe enough in all conscience, but involving an eighteen mile route march back to the car. The day I traversed these hills they were dipping in and out of mist. I found it quite hard to work out which were the true summits as it's all so flat: in particular it's very hard to decide which is the top of Mullaghnarakill. But it matters not, for life is wild and beautiful up here.

Beenmore and Drung Hill form a lovely double mountain and there's a simple if heathery route south off it. If you do have a second car and go down the north side of Drung Hill you will see four highways. The highest is a Christian route of pilgrimage. Not far below it is the old coach road. In the eighteenth century road builders loved to build in a straight line, whatever the terrain. And here they built one over a shoulder that runs straight into the sea. One can easily imagine the terror of travellers in their swaying horse-drawn coaches. Not till the 1850s was the new low road built, with, above it, the railway tunnelling through the hillside. That line was taken up in the 1950s like so many others.

You are here in the kingdom of Drung. Feidlimd, king of Munster, gave the area that stretches from here east to Lough Leane to the daughter of Gulide for making 'a very fair speech'.[1] That was towards the end of the fourth century. It was a small barren kingdom, but it was able to give the king of Kerry a tribute

117

Coomasaharn Lake

of thirty oxen, for which Drung received in return three Swords and three Ships. Not a bad exchange! The kingdom had disappeared by the thirteenth century. My small trip through the kingdom of Drung took only four and a half hours.

6. Knocknadobar

Of all the Kerry hills, Knocknadobar is freshest in my memory. That is simply because I was on its top four weeks ago to the day: my first ascent. The massif is a surprising ninety miles away from Derreen: Thus we had six hours in the car getting there and back. To spend a day driving in Kerry is to waste it. As Lloyd Praeger puts it 'You are always leaving the view behind.' He goes on to recommend a car with a maximum speed of 10 mph which is guaranteed to break down every five miles.

I had seen the unlovely whaleback of Knocknadobar six years earlier, when I was staying at Glencar. But now as we drove towards it my brother Andrew noticed Stations of the Cross marked up it, and our spirits rose as we drove through Cahirciveen with its huge church. Cahirciveen is a considerable town, yet before 1815 it had only five houses. Now, besides the church, it has a turf-fuelled power station which Barrington considers 'wildly extravagant'.

We drove up the steep valley that ends at the pretty little harbour of Coonanna. And then set off up the hill at the spot marked Holy Well. This is dedicated to St Fursa. He was a notable Irish missionary who died at Peronne in 650. His visions of heaven and hell had a deep effect on those later visionary works that culminated in Dante's Inferno. Today the waters of the well are said to cure blindness.

We found St Fursa's at once, and then proceeded uphill to the Stations of the Cross. We had just enquired of their whereabouts from a farmer, and he'd told us that we could not miss them as the nuns had just painted them all white. As we went higher up the hill we could not find them, and began to think that they were perhaps all clustered round the huge summit cross that we had seen from the road.

The route lay up a great stickleback ridge and was a grand painless way to gain height. Then it flattened and we saw ahead the Stations. The lowest one was marked XI. We had therefore missed numbers I to X. We swung onto the top in high spirits, thinking how suitable it was to climb a holy mountain in Holy Week. The summit cross is of Celtic design and quite magnificent. It has a grand air of permanence about it that the iron cross on Carrauntoohill lacks.

And so we had lunch. It was cold and windy, and we returned by the route of penitence. It is not that easy to find all fourteen Stations. There is no track. The only guide, unfortunately, is a considerable litter trail left by the visitors. And the nuns have only painted the fronts of the Stations; the backs are a dark grey and merge with the hillside. However, we did visit all fourteen, and it struck us that it was greatly preferable to ascend by the route we had chosen. The crosses were positioned to give the worst possible ascent – as an additional penance, presumably. When we reached the First Station we were only 30 yards from St Fursa's well. We marvelled at our blindness on the way up: we should surely have sprinkled well water over our eyes.

Knocknadobar by this route is an excellent three hour trip, in no way a slog and in all ways worthwhile. Sean O'Suilleabhain in his *Hill Walks: South West*[7] gives other routes, including the traverse of the whole massif from the Holy Well to Kells. And there's a fine-looking walk over the cliff to the right of Glendalough down to Roads. Once here, however, you should continue east to Kells and not attempt to backtrack along the shore west, as Knocknadobar falls straight into the sea over cliffs.

Surely, though, the point of the Holy Hill is to climb it by the Holy Way. The Stations were built in 1885 by the redoubtable Canon Brosnan of Cahirciveen. He had a church on the slopes of this hill whose roof blew off every winter. But one winter it stayed put, and the good Canon was so grateful that he erected the Stations in thanksgiving. The big cross near the summit is still called the Canon's Cross.

The Canon's greatest monument is without doubt the O'Connel Memorial Church in Cahirciveen: Daniel O'Connel's birthplace. The Canon was determined to commemorate the centenary of Daniel's birth. But there was little money in Iveragh so the Bishop of Kerry turned down the Canon's church as an extravagance. Undaunted, Canon Brosnan appealed to the Archbishop of Cashel, who also refused him. Still undaunted he went to Italy and obtained from Pope Leo XIII both permission and a foundation stone. The Pope ordered the reluctant Archbishop to lay the first stone and start the work. The church was built of Newry granite amidst a sea of financial troubles, including the bankruptcy of the builder. Its spire was never completed.

The great Canon Brosnan also steers me conveniently to Dingle, for in 1868 he persuaded the Bishop of Kerry, David Moriarty, to celebrate mass on top of Brandon Mountain. That service was attended by 20,000 pilgrims. They had all climbed up Brandon the hard way, from Cloghane, and that is the first walk I will describe in Part III.

Dingle

A trip to Dingle is a trip abroad. Its culture and language are foreign to the rest of Kerry. Here the people speak Irish. They are the descendants of the pagan Corcoduibne tribe. That name comes from Corc, first King of Munster (after whom is named Cork city) and his wife Duben. King Corc was in turn descended from the Fir Bolg, or Belgae, who came to Ireland between 500 and 300 BC. This could be the land of Tir na nOg, the island of eternal youth where Oisin and his bride Naimh sojourned for 300 years. You will point out that Dingle is part of the mainland, but I say that Dingle is an island in every sense save the literal. The area is quite cut off from the rest of the country by the barrier of the Slieve Mish mountains. And that range is more isolated than the hills of Iveragh or Beara, for whereas the last two merge gently into the high moorland of Derrynasaggart or Boggeragh, the Slieve Mish plunge into a bog at their landward end. The ground to north, east and south of them is only a few feet above sea level. In the days of Oisin it was not drained and was probably no more than an archipelago of marshy islands. Then the only way to Dingle would have been by sea.

The best place to stay is certainly Dingle town, which once had its own currency. Now it accepts punts. It is still a busy port and has a plethora of the best seafood restaurants I have ever come across. The people of this town speak English or Irish with equal fluency. In the shops we could buy newspapers in English, like the *Kerryman* or the *Cork Examiner*, but that was all. Contrast that to the Glencar Hotel in Iveragh where the *Financial Times* arrives at mid-day and there is even a teleprinter for London stock exchange prices.

The peninsula is thirty miles long and twelve across. The

121

DINGLE – West Of The Connor Pass

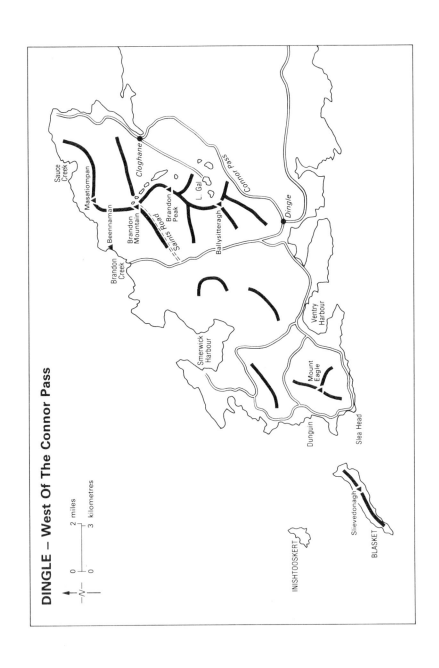

Dingle – Brandon Peak

structure of its hills is most simple. They form a 'L' with Masatiom-pan and Brandon on the vertical, the Connor Pass in the angle, and the Slieve Mish on the horizontal. The hills are higher than Beara's. Bautregaum, Beenoskee and Stradbally are all around the 2,700 foot mark. Brandon rises to 3,127 feet and is Europe's westernmost Munro. Mount Eagle and the Blaskets are even further west. The Blaskets are 'the nearest parish to America', that 'Other World' discovered by St Brendan.

Dingle has a magnificent number of sandy beaches. Since most of the hill walks are short, it's grand to end up the day's exercise with a swim off Castle Gregory or Inch. Tralee Bay and

The Blasket Islands

Castlemaine Harbour are warm, but the further west you go, the colder its gets. I remember finding a delightful strand called Wine Cove. No one else was swimming there, and we soon found out why! At Coumeenole Strand, west of Mount Eagle, the water is cold, but the main challenge is the waves, so huge that no ordinary swimming is possible. This is said to be a dangerous beach, but it's safe enough to wade in waist deep and let the mighty rollers break over you, and maybe knock you flat.

It seems logical to describe Dingle in five sections: The Islands; West of Brandon; Brandon; Dingle to Inch; and the Slieve Mish.

1. Dingle's Islands

The road skirting Mount Eagle is signposted only in Irish and gives a fine view of Great Blasket, and the little island of The Tearaght rising from the sea in a fashion most sheer and dramatic. The Tearaght formed the background to many a scene in the film 'Ryan's Daughter'. We saw the remains of the filming littered about in 1978: a gravel road that led nowhere, and, believe it or not, fibreglass rocks. Why did the film company have to make extra rocks in an area with a surfeit of rock? On that film my friend Paddy Carey, who made 'Oisin' and 'Beara', was second unit cameraman. Paddy came to blows with the producer about sham rocks and there is no tribute to him in the film's credits. But his work is still there: a wonderful time-lapse shot of cloud building up on the Reeks, and another scene of Mullaghanattin lowering a wicked red. It looks like Valhalla in flames.

But I have digressed over to Iveragh and must return to Dingle's islands.

You can travel to Great Blasket from Dunquin Harbour. The ferry is a bright red motor boat. If you are more adventurous though, you will go in a naomhog. These are black canoes of tar and canvas, and the direct descendants of the hide-covered boat in which St Brendan crossed the Atlantic. It is a comical sight to see the fishermen launch them, upended like great beetles with three or four pairs of legs sticking out beneath them. They are similar to Galway's curraghs, but they are bigger and have high stems out of the water.

The Great Blasket is a spine of volcanic rock four miles long and nearly a thousand feet high. All of these islands are igneous, and emanate from the old volcano at Clogher Head. It is quite easy to land on, in contrast to Innishtooskert and Inishvickillane which are as difficult as Beara's Bull Rock. Here were wrecked some of the great ships of the Spanish Armada.

On 25 September 1588 the *Trinidad* was tossing around here as was the Armada's flagship the *San Juan de Portugal* with Admiral Recalde aboard. The *Trinidad* was never seen again, but the flagship managed to anchor east of Great Blasket; a formidable piece of seamanship. Rumour had it that there was a Dingle man aboard.

Admiral Recalde had five men a day dying of thirst. He sent a boat to the mainland for water, but her crew were killed by the English. Other ships joined the group east of Blasket. At mid-day on 1st October the *Santa Maria de la Rosa* came through the sound with her sails torn to ribbons. She was firing her guns for help, but hit the rock called Stromboli and sank at once 'about two splices of cable from the flagship'.[1] Then the *San Juan de Ragusa* came in with her mainmast gone, and she too started to settle in the terrible tides. But Admiral Recalde in his flagship *San Juan de Portugal* made it back to Spain. Four days after his return he died in Corunna.

No one lives on the Blaskets today, though in 1937 the islands still had a school. Lloyd Praeger tells of a visit there, which he describes as fine, provided one is content with a diet of oatmeal and herring. He was collecting rare snails and tells how the schoolchildren thought that he wanted every snail on the island and inundated his cottage with them.

The Blasket islanders spoke only Irish. A literary tradition grew up here: 'From the uttermost part of the peninsula came the last brilliant flame of a doomed society.' In 1925 Thomas O'Criomthain published in Irish his biography of a Blasket Islander, *An tOileánach*. This was followed in the thirties by Muiris O'Suilleabhain's *Fiche Blain ag Fas* (translated as *Twenty years a-growing*[8]) and in the 1940s Peig Sayers wrote *Peig*,[6] which is translated under the same title.

Both *Peig* and *Twenty years a-growing* make compulsive reading: particularly the latter. Muiris O'Suilleabhain's book is not easily put down. He shows up the Western European man, like myself, who yearns after the simple life of the hills as basically a bogus man with inverted values. The real thing – life on the Blaskets – was tough indeed and there was no nonsense about conservation. Puffins' eggs were fair game for the cooking pot. Muiris's idea of the height of civilisation was the flashing neon sign of the Capitol Cinema in Dublin: the sort of thing we go to Ireland to get away from. He must be right. We must be wrong.

You can buy the Blasket Books in the Literary Café in Dingle, for the literary tradition is still thriving. Con O'Neill tells of meeting an islander who addressed him, surprisingly, in English.

'Dere be a lot of otters hereabouts,' said he.

'No. Not otters. There's no fresh water. You means seals,' replied Con.

'Otters,' persisted the Blasket man.

'Seals,' barked back Con.

'No. Otters: dem dat writes books,' said he.

The last islander left Great Blasket in 1955.

2. Dingle West of Brandon

The plain that stretches from Smerwick to Ventry Harbours enjoys better weather than the high hills that bound it to the east. Many a day have I spent here watching the warm air blow in from the Atlantic and forming cloud as it is forced to climb over the great wall of Brandon.

In the south-west corner rises Mount Eagle; you can walk up it in an hour or so from Kildurrihy. You aim for the television mast to the north of Eagle lake and continue up a green road that zig-zags steeply up the shoulder beyond. That green road connects with a turf-cutter's road which runs along the summit ridge and ends amongst workings only five minutes away from the summit, where there is a trig. point.

Mount Eagle

The view of the Blaskets must be beyond compare. I say 'must be' because the day we were there we were in mist. From the summit trig.point it would be fine to continue down to Slea Head. Sean O'Suilleabhain recommends another gentle route from Ballyferriter that takes in also the more northerly peak of Croaghmartin (1,331 ft).

The area is rich in remains both pagan and Christian. There's many a beehive hut and the splendid (though later) Gallarus Oratory.

On the north shore lies tiny Brandon creek, whence St Brendan the navigator set sail for the 'Other World'. It is a foul harbour to sail from if there's even a suggestion of north in the wind. When Tim Severin of County Cork repeated Brendan's voyage in 1977 his ship was stuck here for three days.

There is a confusion of names: why *Bran*don if the Saint's name was *Bren*dan? The answer lies in the legend of Bran. For Bran was the most famous of the pagans who voyaged into the Atlantic. He travelled for years among the magical western isles and spent one year on the Island of Women. When he returned to Brandon Point one of the party, Nechtan, collapsed into a heap of dust. Bran and the others set sail once more and were never heard of again.

So Brandon Mountain is probably called after Bran, not Brendan. And this raises a further question: was St Brendan the first man to reach America? Probably, he was. The legend of Bran is part of a series of journeys called the Imrama, usually involving a trip into the western ocean. The voyage of Maelduin is in the same genre. They are journeys into the Other World, and most likely journeys of the mind, or visions. If you ask a Christian today where heaven is he will point upwards: but the pagans thought that the Life Hereafter lay to the west.

As for St Brendan, Tim Severin has shown that such a voyage was technically possible. He rebuilt the saint's boat in a Cork shipyard. It was quite authentic: a timber frame lashed together and covered with hides. And when he finally cleared Brandon Creek he took two seasons to reach America, leapfrogging by way of the Faroes and Greenland much as St Brendan describes in his 'Navigatio'.

Thus Brandon Creek is mis-named: it should be Brendan Creek.

It is quite hard to find, for most of the English signposts on the plain have been torn down. But it is worth the trip. A couple of naomhogs lie on the quay. To the east there is a remarkably fine cliff walk up to Beennaman. To hear the sea 'shouting against the cliffs' means staying fairly low. The most dramatic part of this walk is in the first few hundred yards, where you can look into green grottoes and black fissures, and where the spray from the biggest waves pours over you. As you gain height the sea becomes more remote. 'The bigger the cliff the greater the drama' does not hold good, at least when you are on top of it. 1,200 feet up is a bit like being in a plane. But 100 feet up, or fifty feet up: that indeed is an awesome experience.

There must be rock climbing up the sea cliffs. The difficulty once again is in landing with a twenty foot swell. Nearly 100 years ago H.C. Hart[4] found a solution to that: it is to undress in the boat and swim to the cliffs trailing a rope. Once lodged on a ledge you haul your gear up, get dressed, and can embark on a 'grand day's sport' known as the Half Tide Race. The idea is to land at half ebb tide and make as much horizontal distance as possible before the tide comes in again. It is bad form to climb above the high water mark. You must stick to the wet rocks, and if forced to take to the water 'excellent practice and much amusement is obtainable in this way, and the slippery nature of the rock teaches sureness of foot'.

Hart's friend Mr Dykes, 'the finest clifter in Houth', beat Hart on one of these races. He led all the way, and shouted back to Hart encouraging things like 'Madness', 'Break your neck', 'You'll never get down'. At the end of the day, though, it was Mr Dykes who was in trouble. He had shed all his clothes and thrown them back into the boat, preparatory to swimming out. Hart then relates with some satisfaction:

> It became at once apparent that a rock exactly in the line of descent was too near the surface. To climb down had always appeared dangerous, on account of the lack of foothold. So an attempt was made on the wall above.
>
> It is marvellous how a naked man can adhere to a cliff. For a full hour an unhappy preadamite man writhed and glued himself against the face of the cliff, descending and re-ascending new lines, but always checked by a straight wall 150 feet up. Anything appeared better than that hateful descent. Some friends ran to a coastguard station a mile or more away for a rope. However before they re-appeared the descent was faced and safely accomplished.

3. Brandon

It was on this mountain that I left the redoubtable Canon Brosnan in Part II. He had 20,000 pilgrims up here. St Brendan had more.

Once he was about to celebrate mass on the summit when he realised that he had forgotten his Bible. He did not have to climb down again to get it, for below him stretched a line of pilgrims filling all four miles of the road to his house. 'My Bible,' he said to the first, and the message went down the line: 'The Saint's Bible . . . The Saint's Bible'. And the Bible came back up from hand to hand.

Many prefer Brandon to Carrauntoohill, for it is on the sea. It is in truth a most typical Kerry hill. A gentle peneplain slopes up from the west. An ice age coum cuts in from the east. The Saint's road starts at Ballybrack and goes up the western shoulder without any difficulty. The route is 'marked' with huge quantities of white paint: the very worst colour to use as it looks like lichen.

At the top is the ruined Oratory whence Brendan and his monks contemplated the Atlantic before setting out. Way down in Beara they will tell you that he did the same from Hungry Hill. Apart from the Oratory, and of course the view if there is one, the top is a nasty place. There's an ugly leaning cross of tubular steel and much litter. St Brendan's Well is full of sweet papers.

To climb Brandon by this route takes only three and a half hours up and down. However it gives you no idea of the grandeur of the mountain. For that you need to approach from the east.

The Canon Brosnan route starts at Faha. You follow the signposts from Cloghane and park your car above the severe 'S' bend at the upper end of the surfaced road. Here another signpost directs you to a grotto whence a line of three poles leads upward. They bear the legend 'Aire, Cnoc Gear'. It means 'Beware, Dangerous Hill'. It is easy to lose the path.

The way is west by north for half a mile rising to the top of a ridge at 1,570 feet. The path is now clearer and generally westwards, circling round an outlying shoulder of Brandon for a further three-quarters of a mile to 2,000 feet. Here the path turns north-west with sudden spectacular views of the coum containing the paternoster lakes. It contours round the side of the coum for three-quarters of a mile and crosses the jumble of boulders at its head for a steep climb of 900 feet to reach the saddle, which is 2,900 feet. Here there are markers: a rock with a white cross, and another sign 'Beware, dangerous hill'. Then there's an easy ascent south for about a third of a mile to the Oratory at 3,127 feet.

If you look south you will see the lake in which lives 'The Great Carrabuncle'. Exactly which lake is not clear. Hart names Lough Bawn, and Lloyd Praeger Lough Veagh or possibly Lough Geal. That is the only one marked on the map, as Lough Gal. What then is this Carrabuncle? A Lough Ness Monster? Hart,[4] says:

> It appears fitfully at night, glittering like silver in the water with gold and silver and precious stones hanging to it galore. It is partly covered with shells which are lined with gold.
>
> Upon one occasion several men went to the lake at night and dived in oilskins to catch this valuable monster. They did not catch him, but pearl mussels, no doubt shed from the Carrabuncle, are found in the lake.

Five years later Nathaniel Colgan met Hart's informant on the slopes of Brandon. This man had never seen the Carrabuncle, and said that when it appeared it lit up the whole lake and that 'If you

Some of Brandon's 16 paternoster lakes

The Gran Ceol Boulder Field with Brandon Peak beyond it

could only catch it you would get some things of great value that follow after it'.

Both the postman and the publican at Cloghane confirmed its existence, and added that the Carrabuncle only appeared every seven years. So Lloyd Praeger went to Lough Gal five times but 'saw nothing, and the lake was mostly inky black with heavy clouds hanging on the dark cliffs that impend above it'. He goes on to speculate about a similar monster called Carbuncolo, said to exist in the Upper Amazon. He suggests that both Irish and South American monsters bear the same name due to the two countries' close links with Spain. And that the precious stone carbuncle is named after the monster.

As to the existence of the Irish monster, Praeger has this to say:

It has never been seen by the cold critical eye of science, but Matthew Arnold reminds us through the mouth of Empedocles that 'Much may still exist that is not yet believed'.

I have yet to describe the two finest walks over Brandon.

The first lies up its east face and starts at Lough Cruttia. You take the road thither south-west from Cloghane. I went this way with my son Ned in 1978, when he was twelve years old.

Cruttia is a mile long, and above it towers Brandon Peak (2,764 ft) in quite the finest prow of rock that I have seen in Kerry. The walk is similar to that up Mangerton's Horse's Glen. It is a series of steps from lake to lake. Whereas in Mangerton's case there are only three lakes, here there are sixteen in the chain. To gain each lake means scrambling up a steep ledge, sometimes of broken boulder, sometimes of living rock. All the way a huge cliff soared up to our left, and ahead of us Brandon threw out an eastern spur with a needle-sharp ridge like those of the Reeks. It was, clearly, another line of nunataks: rocks that had stood clear of the great glacier and been shattered by frost. The remains of a hill fort rise above the nunataks. It is called Benagh.

We traversed a large scree field. This is Gran Ceol which could mean 'Grain Music' or perhaps 'Ugly Music'. The music is made by the boulders that tumble down the cliff in a storm. Then we struck the Faha route, and a steep haul of 900 feet got us to the col. The advantage of any approach from this side is the magnificent view over the Blaskets that opens up as you breast the crest. That day was a hot, thirsty one. We looked forward to a drink from the Holy Well, but when it came to the point we could not face its toffee paper waters and we swung away gently north to Masatiompan. We had lunch and a drink by Lough Duff.

I'm not sure that I'd recommend this northern traverse. There are several minor summits to cross before Masatiompan. That is a very fine conical peak: but there is no view of its northern cliffs from the top, so we dropped down due north and soon found ourselves on dangerously steep ground, but still without a view of the cliffs. Masatiompan's north face is convex. It seemed foolhardy to drop down yet more – we could have skidded a couple of thousand feet into the Atlantic – so we turned east for Sauce Creek which the Guidebook told us had particularly fine sea cliffs. Here again, we could not see much of them. I still believe that the best point to see the cliffs is from Brandon's Creek, further west. There

Masatiompan

they make a formidable barrier and show dramatically why there cannot be a coast road round the north of the peninsula. We dropped down to the hamlet of Brandon, in Brandon Bay. We anticipated hitching a lift, at least as far as Cloghane, but there was no traffic. In Cloghane itself we saw our first car and enquired whether the driver was heading south. 'I'm not heading anywhere,' was the reply. 'The battery has packed up; I wonder, could you give me a push back up the hill?'

Four times we pushed that hateful vehicle up the hill, without success, and then we took our leave. The next car we saw was our own. We had thus finished the day with a seven mile road walk. Climbing boots are peculiarly uncomfortable on tar; it is better to keep to the grass verge. Our trip was of eight hours.

An even finer trip is the traverse of the Brandon Range from the Connor Pass. You will need two cars: the first at the top of the Connor and the second in Ballybrack, unless, of course, you do not mind a bit of roadwork at either end, in which case you can walk the whole journey from Dingle itself. But we started from the Connor. It's an easy 700 feet up to Beennabrack over springy turf: and we hardly noticed the traverse on to Ballysitteragh. Then, though, there is a setback. The col to the north of Ballysitteragh is as low as the Connor Pass, so we lost all the height we had gained. Next follows the main slog of the day, up to the southern summit of Brandon Peak, called Gearhane. That takes one and a half hours.

From Gearhane to Brandon Peak (2,764 ft) the ridge is fine and narrow, with sheer drops to the east. There's even a sign of a path. On Brandon Peak we looked down to a col of 2,000 feet, and a most convenient landmark: a wall contouring up Mount Brandon. Thus, provided Brandon Peak is clear of mist, there can be no route-finding difficulty to Brandon Mountain. Moreover, all along the route, it is obvious that there's an easy escape westwards should a blizzard or worse develop. The only possible danger point is a cliff to the west of Gearhane.

As we came steeply off Brandon Peak we saw for the first time the sheer scale of its cliffs: so vast that it's impossible to include the full height of them in any photograph taken from that point. As we climbed up towards Mount Brandon's wall we went into the mist. We followed the wall around, expecting to cross a very obvious 'Saints' Road', but we never found it and doubled back to achieve the summit.

Heading then south-west by compass we went forever downward without clearing cloud, and still we could not find that holy road. At 1,500 feet we cleared the cloud and met a shepherd who told us that the road was further south. So we tended that way and found a marker cairn. But then we lost the 'road' again. There are sundry cairns dotted over the hillside, but not to any pattern that we could discern. Occasionally we were on bare earth and stone, and the unsightly accompaniment of litter. But then the next moment we were in long untrodden heather. The Saints' road is no more than an uncairned track, discernible in a few places. Only at 500 feet, when we were practically in the village of Ballybrack, did a proper path develop. Thus the Saints' road *ascent*, which we have never done, is really quite dangerous, for there is

Brandon's summit cairn

no hope of keeping to it after the first quarter of a mile. A compass is a must for Brandon.

The traverse took us just under six hours. The total ascent is a surprising 3,400 feet. This route gives the best chance of fine views westward, for the various cols should be clear of mist even if the summits are shrouded.

And so I leave Brandon with regret; for it is a mountain of which one never tires. How good it would be, for instance, to do the traverse from the Connor Pass and then swing down to Faha. And how about a traverse east along the nunatak spur? And a direct assault up the east face of Brandon Peak? All of these we must do when we next visit the Holy Mountain.

We returned to Dingle after our Brandon climb and an invigorating swim. The car was warm. We had a Gilbert and Sullivan tape playing. And we looked forward to a fantastic meal at Doyle's Seafood Bar. And I thought that if Heaven was like this in no way would one be able to fault it, even after an eternity. Why did Bran think that Heaven lay over the Western Ocean, when the real Heaven lay beneath his feet?

4. Dingle to Inch

This area has six peaks of over 2,000 feet. The finer summits however, are in the 1,500 foot range.

The next day saw us back at the top of the Connor Pass, set to walk east of it and circuit Coumanare. The name means 'Valley of the Slaughter'. Recently archaeologists have discovered yew objects buried in the turf – they could have been arrows – but nowhere is there a record of the slaughter itself.

From the top of the Connor to Slievanea (2,026 ft) is hardly any sweat, since the ascent is only 700 feet and there's a road. We looked down on Pedlar's Lake, and the 'high-heel and handbag' brigade who walk up to it from the Connor. Ahead of us lay an extensive peneplain with multiple bog burst. I used to think that these were caused by erosion, but I am no geologist. Lloyd Praeger was both geologist and botanist, and it is worth quoting Praeger on the bog burst, I think:

In certain conditions the lower layers of a bog may become so highly charged

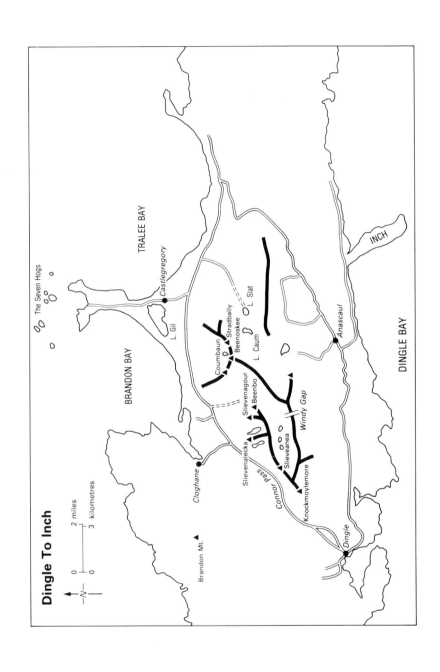

Dingle To Inch

N

| 0 | 2 miles |
| 0 | 3 kilometres |

Brandon Mt. ▲

Cloghane ●

The Seven Hogs

L. Gil

Castlegregory ●

TRALEE BAY

BRANDON BAY

Coumbaun ▲

Stradbally ▲
Beenoskee ▲

L. Slat

L. Caum

Slievenalecka ▲

Slievenagour ▲
Beenbo ▲

Connor Pass

Slieveanea ▲

Windy Gap

Knockmoylemore ▲

Dingle ●

Anascaul ●

INCH

DINGLE BAY

A bog burst

with water that under the pressure of the superincumbent mass they gush out at the lowest point of the floor, dragging the wreck of the more solid upper layers after them. If the bog be large and deep a great flood of semi-liquid matter is ejected, and should the slope below the point of ejection be steep, a devastating torrent may result. That flood leaves behind it a deposit of black turf averaging 3 feet in thickness, contrasted by its black colour with the grassland or other surface. The centre of the area is swept bare to the gravelly drift on which the bog has rested. Near the edges heather covered floes lie about, getting more numerous and closer together till the margin of the firm bog is reached, where the cracks can be seen in all incipient stages.

I have never seen the bog actually bursting, and the torrent of turf sliding downhill. It must be a frightening spectacle, akin to lava flow from a volcano. People can be killed by bog slides. Praeger mentions the case of a family of eight who were carried away and buried by the burst, along with their house and all their livestock. He goes on to point out that the turf debris never lies for long in the valleys, for the farmers use it all for fuel.

Slievenalecka

Now our route lay downward to Slievenalecka, a fine promontory of a peak with precipitous faces to east and west. We had
seen this mountain from Cloghane and it looked a veritable
aiguille. But the walk up the back of it is easy enough. We walked
on to Slievenagour and Beenbo and then dropped south to traverse
the mouth of the valley at 1,100 feet. South of that the whole spur
ending in Knockmulanane was in mist. We went west on a
bearing, and cleared the cloud at Windy Gap. (There are two other
'Windy Gaps' in Iveragh.) Then we climbed back into the cloud,
and stayed so for some time with my son Ned making the normal
discouraging remarks like, 'We crossed this bit twenty minutes
ago: we're going round in circles.'

We were on another area of bog burst. Traversing an unknown
area in mist is an act of faith with the map, not strengthened by the

Waterfall under Slievenagour

Windy Gap (Dingle)

certain knowledge that the map-makers have never been up here and may have missed lakes, or worse, cliffs. We tended a bit too far south and came out of the mist on the shoulder of Knock-moylemore. It was good to see Dingle Harbour spread out below us and the Connor Pass ahead, but whilst we looked the cloud grew blacker and lower. Soon we could see the pass no more, so we went due west from our hill into the bottom of the Ballybowler Valley. From here we had to climb up again to gain the road south of the pass. We trudged up it in inky black weather. A few disappointed trippers drove past with their headlights on. It rained gently. And so we gained the top and drove down; the cloud was now at 500 feet and nothing could be seen of our five and threequarter hour walk.

Beenoskee from Slieveanea

143

Glanteenassig

It's a fine enough trip, though I tend to agree with C.W. Wall[10] that the best of it is over those three splendid tops of Slievenalecka, Slievenagour and Beenbo. The more southerly return is a bit flat.

It will be obvious from the map that the circuit of Beenoskee and Stradbally makes a fine day. The map is right. We left our car in Stradbally village. I asked a farmer the name of the hill ahead, suspecting that he would say something other than Beenoskee. He said 'Binoskwi': not far off the map version.

We gained Stradbally's summit (2,627 ft) and circled round to 'Binoskwi' (2,713 ft). We had an inspiring view of the cliffs above tiny Lough Acummeen. We looked north beyond Rough Point to those curious flat islands, the Seven Hogs of Magharee. Unfortunately we could not see the huge crags dropping to the head of

Glanteenassig Valley to the east. That is a fierce coum and a day or two later we went up it in heavy rain. The wildness of Loughs Caum and Slat is lessened, a bit, by Forestry Commission planting. East of that coum is Glen na Gealt, the Madmen's Glen, where the afflicted came to drink at the well and eat the cresses that grew beside the stream as a cure.

Our descent was heathery, over Coumbaun and trig. point 1,259.

That little four and a half hour walk left plenty of time for a swim and a trip out to Lough Gill with its hundreds of Bewick swans.

South of the Binoskwi circuit lies Lough Anscaul. The glen that holds it has cliffs awful and threatening. Sean O'Suilleabhain recommends a horseshoe route, climbing steeply up Knockmulan-ane (1,953 ft) to the west, thence over the plateau and down the east side over the 1,750 ft Dromavally, shown as Gallain . . . on the half inch map. A green road continues north from the 'Scenic Car Park' by the lough. This can be followed over into Stradbally forest in the north-east, or down to the Glenahoo river north-west. Either of those two routes would achieve a south-north traverse of the peninsula at a fairly lower level. Two cars might be a necessary luxury! The day we were there it really was very wet. We got up to the lip of the plateau where mist and hail confounded us; then we beat an undignified retreat.

It was in Lough Anscaul that Scal Ni Mhurnain drowned. She was a maiden who, when threatened with kidnap by a giant, appealed for help to the mighty warrior Cuchulain, and for a whole week he and the giant stood on opposite sides of the valley hurling boulders at each other. Eventually Cuchulain gave a mighty groan and fell. The maiden took the fatal plunge, and there are three rocks atop Cuchulain's 'boulder firing point' (the hill of Dromavally) called Leaba, Tigh and Uaigh, meaning respectively (Cuchulain's) bed, house and grave.

But Cuchulain was far from dead. He will make more havoc in the next chapter. . . .

5. The Slieve Mish Mountains

The Slieve Mish look like a blunt spearhead on the map, facing

145

Dromavally: the giant Cuchullain's 'Boulder firing point'

east. As they go further inland so they get lower. Thus they fall from the considerable peak of Baurtregaum (2,796 ft) to the tiny hummock of Mountnicholas (512 ft), which makes the end of the 'island' of Dingle. Beyond it lie flat soggy fields. Slieve Mish means the Mountain of Phantoms, and there is more legend attached to this range than to any other.

The most obvious circuit is over Caherconree and Baurtregaum. We left our car about a mile east of Camp and slogged up Gearhane (2,423 ft). That brought us to a broad sweeping ridge straddled by the massive rock called Fionn Mac Cumhaill's Chair (Fionn was the giant who created the Isle of Man); thence onwards to that most legendary of hills: Caherconree. We decided to drop down to look at the fort on its west shoulder. This is a promontory fort, protected on three sides by cliff, and on the fourth by a great wall. The wall is mainly a natural formation of rock and boulder, and the approach to it is somewhat treacherous over hidden fissures in the rock. This was the stronghold of Curoi MacDaire. Whenever a stranger appeared Curoi made his wall spin. He was thus quite impregnable. When three Champions of Ulster came to visit Curoi, he set them the task of spending a night beyond the wall. Then Curoi changed into a demon, and two of the champions, Laegaire and Conall, were so afraid that they jumped inside the wall. But the third champion, Cuchulain, proved quite fearless and kept post till morning. Cuchulain and Curoi then became allies. Cuchulain was laying siege to a Manx chieftain's castle. Curoi now showed him the trick of how to take it, and they agreed that his reward should be the Manxman's daughter, Blathnaid. The Castle fell, but Cuchulain did not keep the bargain. A furious Curoi then seized everything in the castle; jewels, silver, gold and cattle as well as Blathnaid.

Cuchulain the Ulster champion now chased Curoi through Ireland in high dudgeon. When he reached Cashel, Curoi was waiting in ambush. He seized the Ulsterman, buried him up to the neck in sand, shaved his head, and put a cow pat on it. Cuchulain waited for his hair to grow again in silent fury. A year later he arranged a tryst with Blathnaid whose aim was the murder of Curoi. Blathnaid co-operated. Barrington gives as the cause of her treachery the cold climate of Curoi's fort, 2,000 feet high. 'Blathnaid', he says 'was fed up and very wet.'

So Blathnaid set about deceiving her husband. The wall, she said, should be built of much bigger stones: it was unimpressive

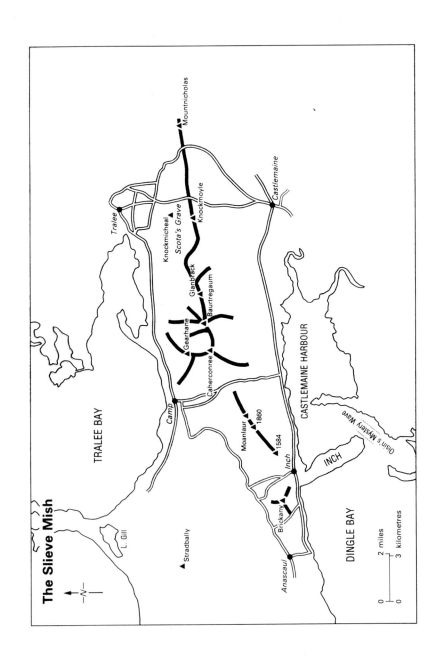

The Slieve Mish

N

TRALEE BAY

L. Gill

▲ Stradbally

Camp

Gearhane ▲
Caherconree ▲
Glanbrack ▲
Baurtregaum ▲

Knockmicheal ▲
Scota's Grave
Knockmoyle ▲

Tralee

Castlemaine

Moanlaur ▲
1860

1584 ▲

Inch

INCH

CASTLEMAINE HARBOUR

Brickany ▲

Anascaul

DINGLE BAY

Oisín's Mystery Wave

Mountnicholas ▲

0   2 miles
0   3 kilometres

with small ones. Would Curoi, therefore, send all his men to haul larger boulders up to the fort? He obliged. Then Blathnaid tipped milk from the Manx Cattle into the Finglas river. It flowed white, a pre-arranged sign to Cuchulain that Curoi was defenceless.

Next, Blathnaid positioned her husband in the gap in the wall and combed his hair. He saw a man approaching, but Blathnaid reassured him that he was a friend, and proceeded to give her husband a bath and put him to bed. She removed his sword. Then Cuchulain burst into the bedroom and murdered Curoi. He took Blathnaid away to Ulster. And that was the end of the Fort of Conree with its magical wall.

We climbed back on to the ridge and swung up the highest of the Slieve Mish: Baurtregaum. The name means 'The Mountain of the Three Hollows'. In truth four coums cut into it, three from the north, one from the south. We had a magnificent view that way of Mullaghanattin and the Reeks in Iveragh.

A finer way up Baurtregaum is perhaps up Derrymore Glen, that big valley that cuts into the massif from the north. Following the true right bank of the river all the way we first came across a ruined watermill, then higher up a series of weirs. Higher still the river divides and we followed the main branch up through a coum as remote as one could wish. At 2,000 feet we reached three tiny lakes, and each of these has also been dammed, though the dams are now breeched. Behind them the cliffs of Baurtregaum soar upward into the mist. The middle lake has a delightful beach of red sand – a fine camping spot. Above the lakes is a hanging valley full of fantastically shaped rocks. One of them is Fionn MacCumhail's Table, and as Sean O'Suilleabhain says, 'A great many other rocks are shouting for a name'. The cascades of the Derrymore River are as fine as any in Dingle.

We went back to Camp, and drove south to Aughills. That road gives the most impressive view of Curoi's fort. The walk, once again, was a short one of five and a half hours. We went back towards Dingle, and stopped for a drink in Anascaul at the South Pole Bar. This is named after Tom Crean, who took part in Scott's tragic expedition to Antarctica.

There's a good walk also to the west of the Aughills Camp road. It is, simply, the traverse of the western Slieve Mish, that is Knockbrack, Mounlaur, Knockmore and trig. point 1,584.

Derrymore Glen. The top lake

We left our car in a quarry opposite Knockbrack and bounced along the ridge, which might be marred by long heather in high summer, but is perfect going in spring. It gives an unrivalled view to both north and south of the peninsula all the way, and takes no more than four hours including the lunch break. We descended over steep scree down to Inch.

Further east the 'Phantom Mountains' are lower, but there's an interesting circuit in Scota's Glen. From Tralee you take the Ballyard road and go straight over the first cross, then left and right at the second. Follow signs up Short Hill saying 'Viewing Park'. It is best to leave your car in a gravel pit near the wood marked on the map as Glanaskageen; then drop down and ford three streams. The large slab let into the rock after the third stream is Scota's

A rock 'shouting for a name' in Derrymore

151

Grave. Scota was a daughter of a Pharaoh and was killed here in 1695 BC. One version has it that she jumped from one side of the glen to the other, like many other mythical figures (the hag of Hag's Glen for instance), and that one day she jumped, unaware that she was pregnant, and fell to her death.

From here you can swing easily up Knockmoyle and over to trig. point 1,814, where you will find the 'Iron Man'. This is a Department of Posts and Telegraphs dish that bounces a microwave link between Limerick and Tralee.

The trip is of five and a quarter miles and should take no more than three hours out and back.

And with that thoroughly pleasant journey you have completed all the finest walks that Dingle has on offer.

Epilogue

The beauty of the Kerry Hills, I said at the start, is that they are wild and unvisited. Now I would refine that statement. The beauty of the Kerry Hills is that they are wild and *were* visited. The tales of Cuchulain and St Patrick, the beehive huts, the magic waves, the Ogham stones; above all the strange feeling on the hills that there are people watching you: little people perhaps, certainly people of a charm and generosity unknown to the present century. Therein lies the mystical attraction of the hills. As I walk across them it is not that I feel a sense of timelessness; I have the feeling more that I have gone back in time 1,000 years. English history started in 1066, but Irish history a thousand years earlier. This is an ancient land of courtesy and scholarship.

The Irish have the gift of the gab, as the saying goes. Certainly they express themselves better than the English, and this is due to their ancient education. An ordinary Irishman 1,000 years ago, would have been equally at ease expressing himself in Gaelic, Greek, or Latin. The Ogham inscriptions are in Latin. That is perhaps why events that seem old to the English are new to the Irish: thus an Englishman claiming that the Cromwellian settlers have been in Ireland 'a long time' is wrong. In Irish eyes the Cromwellians' came yesterday. Even my own ancestors, the Geraldines, are 'settlers' though they came to Ireland in the early thirteenth century.

Far be it from me to comment on Irish affairs; but I will quote what another Irishman (Lloyd Praeger) said of his country in 1937:

Ireland is a very lovely country. There is only one thing wrong with it, and that is that the people that are in it have not the common-sense to live in peace with one another and their neighbours. Past events and Political Theory are allowed to bulk much too large in our mental make-up. The result is dissatisfaction, unrest, and occasionally shocking violence. That 'frontier' which is a festering sore in Ireland's present economy was the gift of an English Government: but Ireland brought it on herself. 'Well now' a Connemara man said to me 'Politics is the devil itself': and in this country that is only too true. If St Patrick had banished from Ireland politics instead of snakes he would have conferred a far greater boon, and this lovely land would have had peace and charity as well as faith and hope.[9]

But what care I for politics when I swing over the hills? When I'm walking I think of other things: natural dangers, natural glory, the fear of mist and treacherous cliff, the glory of the summit gained and the view over coum and cascade to the ocean.

I have in my sitting room two pictures: one of the Cuillins; one of the Reeks. The Cuillins are somehow all wrong. The Reeks are somehow all right. Why is this so? And why in truth do I always compare other mountain ranges to the Kerry Hills and find the others wanting?

The Alps are O.K., I say, but they're too neat. The Scottish Highlands are O.K., but they're too barren. And the hills of Wales and the Lake District are like Hyde Park on a Sunday.

Certainly the hills of Kerry owe much to their isolation. Certainly, too, they were the first hills that I ever climbed. Those two factors contribute to my love of them, but do not explain it. The word that does is, I believe, 'Water'. The Kerry Hills are liquid. Therein lies their magic. Sparkling streams, mighty cascades, black lakes. Water to gaze over, or swim through, or drink. Water, too, underfoot, everywhere. I do not walk over the hills; I squelch over them. That is the mountain sound peculiar to Kerry: the gentle noise of vibram on bog. And the air is laden with water: that's the more subtle magic. It turns the ground underfoot black, brown, grey, pink, and green, and the distant hills an indigo blue.

And so I look again at my two pictures and have my answer. The Cuillins are neatly defined into separate areas; rock in its proper place, likewise scree, and grass, and a lake. But the picture of the Reeks has no defined areas. It is a liquid whole: water in the lakes blending with water on the hillside blending with water in the air. And that gives the hills a softness and a clarity that exists nowhere else on this earth. I have travelled the world. I am not like Father Keegan who 'did not know what his own house was like because he had never been outside'. If I have over-praised Kerry it is not for lack of comparison but because of it.

And so I sit on fair Knockatee, gazing out to St Brendan's magical mystery lands of the west.

Further reading and acknowledgements

1. Barrington, T.J., *Discovering Kerry*, Blackwater Press, 1976
2. Coleman, J.C., *The Mountains of Killarney*, Dundalgen Press, Dundalk, 1975
3. Froude, J.A. *Two Chiefs of Dunboy*, Longmans, Green & Co., 1906
4. Hart, H.C., *Climbing in the British Isles*, Longmans, Green & Co., 1895
5. Mould, Daphne Pochin, *The Mountains of Ireland*, Gill & Macmillan, 1976
6. Sayers, Peig, *Peig: The Autobiography of Peig Sayers of the Great Blasket Island*, P. Talbot, 1974
7. O'Suilleabhain, Sean, *Irish Walk Guides: South West*, Gill & Macmillan, 1979
8. O'Sullivan, M., *Twenty Years A-Growing*, O.U.P., 1983
9. Praeger, Robert Lloyd, *The Way That I Went: an Irishman in Ireland*, Methuen, 1947
10. Wall, C.W., *Mountaineering in Ireland*, Federation of Mountaineering Clubs of Ireland, 1976

Whilst the author is in general indebted to all those listed above for their unknowing help he feels that he must single out in particular first T.J. Barrington, without whose comprehensive work on Kerry's archaeology and legend the author would have been completely lost; and also Sean O'Suilleabhain, who wrote the Irish Walk Guide South West, from which the author has drawn heavily. So, a special thank you to Messrs Barrington and O'Suilleabhain.

Bernd Thee

Bernd Thee on Slievenagour

Bernd Thee was born in 1958 in Altena, Westphalia. He was educated at Laasphe and went on to Siegen University where he read Art and Roman Catholic Religion. His first photographic exhibition was in the Siegen Town Gallery with the theme 'People and Mannequins'.

In 1983 he moved to Dingle and has further exhibited frequently in 'Tigin Ban', Dingle's own art gallery.

He lives in Ventry with his wife Marina and his son Oliver, who was born on 18 March 1986.

Index